7295

915.0442

Salisbury, Charlotte Y
    Asian diary, by Charlotte Y. Salisbury. New York,
Scribner [1968, °1967]

    158 p. illus., map, ports. 21 cm.

1. Asia—Descr. & trav.   I. Title.

915.0442 S167a
DS10.S3   915'.04'42   68–11360

    Library of Congress   [5]

Asian Diary

ASIAN DIARY

by Charlotte Y. Salisbury

CHARLES SCRIBNER'S SONS · NEW YORK

Printed in the United States of America
Library of Congress Catalog Card Number 68-11360

PICTURE CREDITS: NOS. I, 5, 13, 17, 19 BY THE AUTHOR;
NO. 12 BY HARRISON E. SALISBURY; ALL OTHERS
BY HARRISON E. SALISBURY FOR The New York Times

for Harrison

☙ one

May 16, 1966, New York City, 7 a.m.

IT IS hard to leave: With all the excitement and anticipation over our trip—to places I never dreamed of seeing and to which Harrison has never been—there is so much here, and so many people I am not used to living without. I couldn't sleep after five so got up and wrote letters about the house in Roxbury; my will; left checks for the household expenses made out to the middle of July; locked up the silver. Scott and Rosina and Steffy are going to drive us to the airport. Leaving for a trip like this is not easy for me; I worry about everything—the cats, burglars, the furnace, fire, things breaking, the fact that Scott and Rosina may go into the Peace Corps before we get back and then what. They are in charge of the house and if they do get their orders will have to find someone to take care of every-

7

thing. But it isn't easy. Well . . . . . I am waiting for all these worries to fall off; they should cease to loom so large in the excitement and changes in the days ahead.

May 17, Honolulu Airport, 12 noon Hawaii time
(6 p.m. New York time.) Waiting to
board the plane to Tokyo.

We ARRIVED at midnight this time (6 a.m. New York time) and spent the remainder of the night at the Hotel Moana. We had breakfast on the edge of Waikiki Beach which is much more beautiful than in pictures. We ate fresh pineapple and watched the green-blue water rolling gently onto the white sand and began to feel we have finally, really, started on this trip which is to take us around China, to as many of the countries on the periphery as we can get to. Harrison never gives up trying to get into China but this is second best, at least. He will talk to as many people as he can and try to find out what is going on inside China, what her neighbors are thinking about, what they think of China and what they think of us.

As we get nearer to South East Asia the war in Vietnam becomes more and more real. This morning we took a drive around Honolulu and we visited the Punch Bowl Cemetery. At one end of this enormous scooped-out crater high above the city stands a huge stone memorial, an angel keeping guard over thousands and thousands of dead young men; dead before they had a chance to live; killed in the wars we have fought on other lands; one section for World War II, one for Korea, and, as our driver put it, "this new section opening up now for Vietnam." It sounded as though he were talking of a new motel or a new dormitory for one of our ever-expanding universities.

I was stunned at those words, and at the sight of all those graves, row after row, all flat stones (they don't have crosses any more as it is impossible for the big mowing machines to cut the grass between them). I thought of Curtis, of Scott, of Mike and Steffy, of all the other boys of all the other mothers in all the other countries. This is the reality of war, of the comfortable "little" war in Vietnam, the "brushfire" war, some of our military call it. How can they? How can they turn our sons into corpses for shipment to this old volcanic crater only ten minutes' drive from the blue surf and white sand of Waikiki?

While we were there two buses drove up and stopped in front of the guardian angel. The doors opened and out spilled a group of tourists—all American, a few men, but most of them women. In their shirtwaist dresses and flat-soled sightseeing shoes they spread out among the graves, scanning the markers, looking for a name, a name made familiar by war, a friend's son, their own son, perhaps, as if they were looking for someone at a cocktail party.

As I watched these women, mothers, grandmothers, sisters, aunts, the inevitable survivors in war or peace, I wondered what they were feeling. Was this just a part of the day's sightseeing, part of the packaged tour? Were they shocked and revolted as we were, or were their feelings deep, obscure, unrecognized even by themselves? Is there perhaps some strange unconscious desire of a woman that she would prefer to know her son is dead, so hers forever, rather than to have him alive and loving someone else? How else do we account for the glory attached to "giving" one's son to the country? What motivates the mothers and the widows who march to martial music, proud of their donation—an able-bodied man blown up or shot to death in unimaginable circumstances?

I cannot understand it. The horror is beyond my comprehension. Such destruction of human life seems to me the most senseless, cruel waste. Surely there must be other ways to resolve our problems.

Later, Tokyo Airport

WE ARE on the Pan American plane waiting to take off for Hong Kong. We transferred from BOAC and I am sorry. The service on our planes is not as courteous and considerate—it is so slapdash and casual. I always feel that if my plane is going to crash I want to hear those lovely English voices saying, "this way, Madame," even if it is into the ocean. From what I could see, landing at Tokyo might have been landing in New Jersey; smoke stacks, oil tanks, smog, smoke, and all the signs in English.

May 19, Hong Kong

COMING down in Hong Kong last night was so beautiful it didn't seem like the same world we had left in Tokyo. Lights on the mountains, ships in the water, twinkling and alluring. I didn't see how it could be as lovely by day, but it seems to be. At the airport we first heard the sing-songy voices of the Chinese, and on the ferry from Kowloon the captain sang out announcements in Cantonese and English. Everyone was going somewhere, even at night; doing something, walking, scurrying, and talking at the same time. From our window here on the twenty-third floor of the Mandarin Hotel the boats in the harbor seem like the people; some chugging back and forth in even pattern, others darting here and there, and occasionally a junk with a colored sail proudly makes her way among the noisy newcomers. The sounds of the city, the harbor and the people come up to us clear and strong, not floating, but exploding into our room as if they had been shot out of a cannon.

May 20

HARRISON was very busy today seeing China-watchers and experts in many fields and I spent the morning looking at the shops and watching the people. The constant movement is fascinating. I know there is a steady stream of activity in New York and other Western cities, but it is never like this. The charm, the color, the intrigue, are missing; perhaps because it is all so familiar. Here everything is strange and I can imagine all sorts of mysterious messages being carried, maybe in the market baskets of the lovely women in their slit silk skirts or black trousers; notes being passed to the friendly shopkeepers; meetings, connivings, plottings on a world-wide scale.

In the afternoon I went on a boat trip around the harbor. I saw the typhoon shelters where thousands of Chinese live on boats tied together and to the wharves. The boats vary in size from large junks to tiny sampans. In the small spaces so many people call home there are parents, children, babies, grandparents, dogs, household paraphernalia, baskets, stoves, flowers in pots. Entire lives from birth to death are lived out here. Children propelled small boats rapidly after us, or swam to the side of our junk hoping for a coin. The typhoon shelters are tucked around corners of the harbor and out of the main traffic, which consists mostly of ferries, small passenger boats, junks, freighters from all over the world, junks from Red China flying their flags of yellow with five red stars, and a few U. S. Navy ships, conspicuous because they were the only warships I saw.

May 21

TODAY I went to the Peak, from which there is such a breath-taking view. Hong Kong surprises me the way Venice did because every thing is more than I had imagined. Views are more spectacular, the high buildings on the mountain sides more fantastic, the mood and feeling of the city more exciting and provocative, the typhoon shelters more extraordinary, and so on; anything I encounter is more than someone has said or written it is.

On my way down from the Peak I visited the Tiger Balm Gardens. This is the creation of Aw Boon Haw, a man who invented and made a lot of money out of Tiger Balm ointment. With the profits he built this labyrinth of steps, tunnels, figures, monsters, flowers, fountains—all climbing up and around the steep side of the hill with a delicate white pagoda on top. In the middle of it all is Aw Boon Haw's grave and on top of that a life-sized statue of him, looking like Lenin in a business suit, gazing out over the harbor.

I wonder how long he will have this commanding post and if Hong Kong will be a free British port until the lease expires in 1997. I don't believe Red China would have much reverence for a capitalist making millions and leaving this bizarre monument to himself. How will the Red Guards treat this memorial? With tenderness and humor? I don't think so.

May 23

YESTERDAY we spent on the water with Seymour and Audrey Topping in their junk. The Toppings live on the other side of the island from Hong Kong and keep their boat in Deep Water Bay. We sailed around the smaller islands, had lunch and stopped for water-skiing and swimming. The sun was hot, the water clear and cool and the outer islands looked the way I imagine some of the Greek islands do, rocky with sparse shrubs and coarse grass.

Beyond these islands lies China, not very far, yet the farthest land in the world from us. It is hard to believe that we can relax and enjoy ourselves so near to people who regard us as enemies. Perhaps we were being watched through glasses or a telescope; perhaps they were suspicious of our innocent recreation. How strange and upsetting; here we are, only a few days out of New York, actually living in the very midst of the problems we think and talk about so much at home.

At sundown we headed for Aberdeen, the typhoon shelter on that side of the island. Here the working fishing junks go out regularly into Communist Chinese waters and return with their catch. Here also are the finest of Hong Kong's floating restaurants and sampan taxis. Sailing toward the shelter we passed many beautiful private houses on hills and cliffs; down below them on the water, tiny sampans and junks, the homes of large Chinese families. Minute houses are built out over the water, like match-boxes stuck onto the rocks with paste.

We dined in the floating restaurant. Millions of lights were draped on the outside and from the inside came the most incredible noise. Fans were blowing on the ceilings and gay lanterns hung on the walls. Every table was full; every group looked as if they were having a special party. Most were Chinese, many with the whole family. I have never heard so much talk, laughter and noise; everyone having a wonderful time. What a contrast between our conception of the Chinese—mysterious, inscrutable, Oriental Dr. Fu Manchus, and these gay, outgoing, friendly, unsubtle people, having such an enormous amount of fun from simple, normal everyday pleasures like taking the family out for a meal. The people inside China must be the same and I wonder how they can make out with a government whose ideals are so puritanical, strait-laced, boring and humorless. There must be many conflicts.

We picked out our fish from a tank, then watched it being prepared by an assembly-line of cooks. A Chinese opera was being acted at one end of the upstairs room where we had dinner; very stylized and odd if one doesn't know what it means. We ate a lot, stayed late and took a sampan taxi back to land. It was fitted out with a straw mat under our feet and straw stools and chairs to sit on. A lovely Chinese girl propelled our boat with the long oar; her little daughter played underfoot, watched over by the grandmother. The husband worked in one of the restaurants.

May 24

WE HAD not expected to go to Cambodia; Bangkok was our next scheduled stop, but suddenly we have Cambodian visas. This is a surprise; diplomatic relations between us and the Cambodians were severed in 1964 and very few Americans are allowed in, except to go to Angkor to see the temples. I wonder what this means. It is close to North Vietnam; perhaps we can go there. This is what Harrison hopes. We left South Vietnam out of our itinerary as it is not pertinent to the point of this trip and I have said over and over that I don't want to go anywhere near Vietnam. I have such a horror of war, such a revulsion at what we are doing there, at the suffering and misery we are inflicting, such a sense of frustration as I watch my country in the role of a huge pompous bully, like Goliath fighting David, ruthlessly bombing a tiny country, alienating people all over the world by our blind and rigid policies, that I can't bear the thought of seeing it. But North Vietnam is different. No American woman has been there and only a few men. Perhaps if we are able to get in we can do some good.

We leave tomorrow so I spent today buying a few presents and walking around trying to see everything. I want to take the feeling of Hong Kong with me. I may never return, or there may not be a Hong Kong to return to.

Who knows from day to day which parts of the world will be free and open and which will be closed tightly to visitors and intruders alike? When I first saw Casablanca several years ago I thought, what strange combinations; women still in veils and men in cheap Sears Roebuck suits. But in Hong Kong there is a more deep sense of things coming together and nothing seems alien. Rickshaws pulled by old men, millionaires in big expensive cars, mansions on the tops of the hills and refugees living in huts on the tops of the buildings; so much modern, so much rich, so much old and so much poor, all woven into the tapestry of life in Hong Kong.

There has never been a city like this—an open port with living and business for everyone; a meeting place where anyone in the world can come; Old China, New China, communists, capitalists, East and West, each individual and fiercely nationalistic, yet each a part of the whole.

 *two*

May 25

    WE ARE flying to Cambodia in a DC6, which I prefer to the big jets. They fly lower and you can see what you're flying over. As we started we could see the coast of China and islands belonging to her, and now we are flying over South Vietnam. It surprises me to see such beautiful lush green country—I had imagined every inch was torn up and scorched by war. I wonder what lurks beneath the green, hidden from our eyes by the thick jungle growth? What torn and mangled bodies lie there rotting in the tropical heat—bodies which lie in such inaccessible places they can never be carried out and flown back to a military cemetery. No mothers, fathers, no one, will ever come to their graves to weep. No child will lay a flower there on Memorial Day; no politician will extoll their bravery for having killed and been killed in a country 10,000 miles away. How baffling to be up here in this comfortable plane, about to have lunch, knowing that directly below men are fighting and dying. It makes me feel crazy, insane. It is so terribly cockeyed.

Later

I HAD champagne for lunch, a little against Harrison's advice. I think he feels nothing alcoholic is best for travelling in these hot countries. I told him about my grandmother who went to Europe every year and immediately after boarding the ship got into her bed and had nothing but champagne and saltines for the entire crossing because she was afraid of being sick and this prevented it.

H. gave me some pearls in Hong Kong—three strands with a gold clasp and earrings to match. They were delivered to me in a pretty silk case just before we left. I never imagined having a necklace like this.

May 26, Phnom Penh, Cambodia

WE ARRIVED here yesterday afternoon and were met by a representative from the Ministry of Information. As we stepped out of the plane I gasped. This is my first experience with South East Asian heat; wet, humid, sticky, boiling heat. We drove to the Hotel Le Royal where we have a big comfortable room with air conditioning and a wonderful man to look after us. We went immediately for a swim in the hotel pool but the water is so hot the only refreshing thing is getting out of it. The Ministry of Information are our official hosts and they have presented us with a schedule so full we won't have an extra minute either to relax or do anything by ourselves. Already today H. has been busy with interviews and we have been taken to the Art Museum and the Royal Palace.

The Art Museum is a huge red building with a large court and wonderful carvings, filled with statues taken from the temples at Angkor, and other places, and objects of art and interest. Our guide, a pretty young girl, lovingly caressed many of the statues, murmuring, "Very beautiful, very beautiful," and we agreed. Many of the statues look like the people we have seen in the streets—small (compared to us), well-formed bodies and beautiful faces. The Royal Palace is a compound of exquisite buildings, each a jewel of gorgeous colors, pinks, yellows, greens, a dream of oriental beauty and grandeur and loveliness. A collection of diamonds and emeralds and fabulous jewelry—all magic to someone from New England. So much exotic beauty is hard to believe and absorb. The royal family does not live here any longer; it is just for business, state functions and show.

May 27

LAST night we dined with Mr. and Mrs. Forain, he French and a close advisor to Prince Sihanouk, she Chinese and exquisite—young, pretty, and very lively. The dinner was Vietnamese and wonderful, as food seems to be in this part of the world; similar to Chinese but crisper and different flavors. Mrs. Forain told me that she hadn't been able to have a baby for five years and Western doctors had said an operation was necessary. She went to a doctor in China who treated her with acapuncture; he put three needles in across her stomach, by the pelvis, and she conceived the next day. She said she had kept track of everything and written down the date. She also said she only had one treatment and it didn't hurt at all, she felt nothing. Harrison says this story proves his theory that many of our physical troubles are really mental or emotional and acapuncture cures that part. Nearly always that is all that needs to be cured.

We talked about the different customs and ways of life in the U. S. and the East. Mrs. F. told me that she and her husband had been staying at the Waldorf several years ago and on arrival, being weary, ordered two Scotch and sodas to be brought to their room. They waited about forty-five minutes and finally a boy appeared with two glasses with Scotch already poured out, and some soda. He plunked it all down and started to go. Mrs. F. said, "Aren't you going to open the soda?" He replied, "Open it yourself in the bathroom," where there was a built-in opener. This would never happen in Asia, or in Europe; only in the United States where we seem to be so afraid of not being equal that we have no notion of service, or sometimes even of doing a job well. It is interesting to note that one of the guests, the product of a communist country, has servants and help with her baby, while I, a capitalist, took all the care of my four children and the household and have always washed my own underclothes. The latter custom, I read somewhere, the Red Guards are trying to initiate in China today.

May 28, Noon

OUR guide has come to our room each morning at seven, banged on the door and told us our schedule for the day. H. usually has interviews starting immediately after breakfast, then for an hour or so before lunch we are taken together to a museum or exhibit of some kind. After lunch, more of the same, so we have packed a lot into these two and a half days. It's easy to see how desperately the Cambodians are trying to keep their country out of war, how worried they are that they will be engulfed or run over by the Vietnamese struggle, and how much they are trying to show us so that we will understand their feelings. I find being an American here is a difficult position to be in, a situation I never imagined I would find myself in. There doesn't seem to be anything to say for this war that makes any sense except to wish it would end.

Every time we walk out of the hotel we are met by a barrage of men with pedicabs. I try to resist them, preferring to walk, but yesterday a young man approached me and said, "You know Mrs. Topping in Hong Kong; I think about her every day," which I couldn't resist. Though I have an aversion to being pushed or pulled by another human being, I found this quite pleasant. Audrey's admirer is a very chatty young man and as he showed me around the city I got a lot of feeling of the streets and the life. Watching these people, who all seem to be beautiful with a natural elegance and style, I feel oversized, gauche and crude. They are exquisite, but not at all fragile; very lean and healthy and strong. Most women wear trousers or the traditional long wrapped skirt, the sampot, but many of the younger girls wear short skirts and tops.

Included in the tour with our guide yesterday was a visit to the Exposition building where we saw fine exhibitions of the arts, crafts and industries, health and education. It is interesting and extraordinary to see what giant steps they have taken in public health in the last ten years. The comparative statistics of numbers inoculated against cholera, etc., are staggering. No wonder Prince Sihanouk is struggling to keep his country neutral. Involvement of any kind in war would mean an end to this sort of progress—a whole shift of emphasis. There was an impressive show of silver work, beautiful knives with ivory handles, carved forks, spoons and gorgeous boxes, platters, cups, etc. The materials, too, were beautiful, cottons and silks, and we saw a show of all the agricultural products with pictures, and cases of the actual grains. I am surprised that so much corn is grown in this part of the world where it is so humid and wet when at home it does best when it is dry.

We went also to Prince Sihanouk's private museum which is really a royal scrapbook collection of personal memorabilia —pictures, medals, presents from other countries, letters from statesmen and kings and movie stars, and upstairs the bedroom furniture of his grandfather, father and mother. The first two were very elaborate, especially the father's, which was beautiful wood inlaid with ivory, but his mother's was very modest, actually middle-class style, no decoration or color; like a maid's room compared to the others.

When we first got here I asked to see a hospital and they have been trying to arrange a visit. We understood it was to be today but as we drove off from the hotel our guide said, "The director of the hospital is unable to see you today so we are taking you to see the nearest thing to a hospital, the alcohol factory." This seemed a strange substitute but there we went, to a fairly large plant of several buildings with huge vats of mash and brine, simmering and boiling in the heat. We watched men making first alcohol, then gin, whiskey and other beverages. In another department pretty girls were making perfume and putting it in bottles with chic French labels. I wonder if things ever get mixed up there, if perhaps some whiskey might end up in a bottle labeled cologne and vice versa. They plan to can orange juice in the near future, which would be good business and good for the general health of the people.

This afternoon we are going to Angkor in our car with our chauffeur and our guide. We will stay three days.

May 29, Angkor

IT TOOK us about five hours to drive here yesterday and we had a wonderful chance to see the country and watch the people. Angkor is over three hundred kms. from Phnom Penh and the road took us through several fairly big towns, small villages and groups of houses. We noticed we were never out of sight of a house until just a few miles from Angkor, where there would be a group of houses, then a stretch of cultivated fields; this pattern repeated until the outskirts of Siem Riep. Generally alongside the road there is a wet garden plot or a water hole and just behind that on drier ground, the house, surrounded by thickly

planted banana or palm trees, encircled by a fence. Houses
are on stilts for several reasons; because of flooding by rain
or the river going over its banks; shelter from the sun and
rain, and storage. In the evening, cows and other animals are
brought from the fields to be shut inside the fence for the
night and most sleep under the house. Fires for cooking are
inches away from the line of the house and large jugs for
catching rain stand at intervals. Where the spaces next to
the road were full of water, they were also full of animals;
the sleek gray water buffaloes soaking with only their noses
showing; enormous black and pink pigs wallowing; small
black and white ducks paddling back and forth like toy
boats and even the little horses, up to their necks, cooling
off. Often the children jumped, dove and swam happily in
the mess. Typhoid, cholera, dysentery, kept coming to my
mind, but I suppose they must be immune to many of the
bacteria that make us so sick.

Until I saw the color I never had imagined such a rich
lush green as the rice paddies. Seymour Topping calls
Cambodia a technicolor country—the greens and blues seem
unreal, they are so brilliant and intense. It is odd we haven't
had any rice since we've been here, only French-fried
potatoes and spaghetti. Between the paddies there is a
contraption hung on a tripod with which one person scoops
water from one paddy to the other. Another method we
saw was two women swinging a box between them which
took the water from one paddy and tossed it out onto the
other with a big splash; each a long slow process, but
perhaps if it were done more quickly it wouldn't suit the
rice as well.

Men and women were going about their daily lives with a

natural dignity and composure rarely seen in our culture. Working around their houses, cooking over fires, carrying babies on their hips, walking to and from the fields with hoes over their shoulders, or sitting on the backs of bicycles holding a baby in one arm and bundles of food, bananas, wood, anything, in the other; balancing everything over bumps, the women seem even more beautiful than in the city. They wear brighter colored sampots, usually with a black top, while in the city they seem to wear more black skirts with a white top. The men wear short pants, usually to just above the knee, and all cover their heads with hats or cloth wrapped around or both.

We were impressed to notice a government school in every town. We saw the children sitting at their desks or playing in the yards and later many were walking or bicycling home. In some schools the girls all dressed alike, white blouses and green or blue skirts, just like schoolgirls anywhere.

As we arrived late and in the dark we first saw Angkor Wat when we walked out of our bedroom at 7 a.m. to meet our guides. The story is that a French naturalist, Henri Mouhot, while searching for specimens in 1860, stumbled on some large stones, looked up and saw this temple. This hotel is supposedly built on the exact spot of his fortunate fall. Angkor Thom had been the capital city during the height of the Khmer power and for the years between 800 and 1200 many temples were built by the kings. Theirs was a highly civilized era and their architecture, sculpture and paintings are among the most beautiful the world has ever known. Though the Khmers were driven out by the Thais and their temples abandoned to the jungles for so many centuries, miraculously a few remain in good enough condition to give us a glimpse into the life of this glorious period in Cambodia's history.

Built of sandstone and brick, the temples rise up out of the jungles or lie hidden among huge trees which have wound their roots around the walls and towers like constricting snakes. The sculptures and bas reliefs show the life as it was in those ancient days; men fighting to defend their borders, fighting to keep their rivers from the invaders, fishing from their graceful boats or from the banks or up to their waists in water, ploughing the land with oxen and water buffaloes, pulling loads of wood. There are women with beautiful serene faces, wearing sampots wrapped as they are today, gossiping in the market, cooking over the fire, carrying baskets of food on their heads, babies in their arms. We saw a scene of a wedding and next a woman in childbirth with a midwife assisting, and children everywhere. It is not much of a step to come out of the temples into the present. In spite of the inevitable encroachings of modern life—cars and buses and roads, cities and noise—the people seem to move along with nature at just the right pace for everything to thrive. Everything is interwoven and meshed together and the colors are from heaven.

May 31, Angkor

WE HAD our first real Cambodian dinner Sunday night and, finally, Cambodian rice, which is lovely and delicate. The menu consisted of big rice puffs on which we put a peppery coconut mixture, a fish patty wrapped and cooked in a banana leaf, chicken cooked in a pot wrapped in lotus leaves, tiny, hot stuffed peppers, rice with everything and dessert made of bean curd and gelatin and eggs, shaped into petals and flowers. Over everything was a contradiction of tastes, a suggestion of a sweet perfumey essence that also seemed to come right out of the earth and rivers —delicate yet pungent, good but repulsive.

We go back to Phnom Penh tomorrow morning early and I am sorry to be leaving Angkor. There is so much here, so much beauty, so many things we haven't been able to see, so much to learn about the history of this lovely little country with its exquisite people.

June 2, Phnom Penh

YESTERDAY afternoon we watched a run-off of a movie which had been made in North Vietnam. The other people watching were the Forains, two children aged ten and twelve, several Cambodians and us, about fifteen in all. The Vietnamese people were shown in the simplicity and beauty of their daily lives, so like the people we have just seen on the trip to and from Angkor. We saw them responding to an air raid alarm—the children running out of schools to shelters, babies in baskets being lowered into holes alongside the roads, factory workers leaving their places to man the anti-aircraft guns, men and girls alike. The American supersonic bombers zoomed across the sky expelling their death-dealing devices. They go so fast there is hardly any warning and it must be impossible for them to take accurate aim. Then we saw the results—the crumbling, smoking remains of houses, schools, churches, as well as areas which are supposed to be singled out as military targets, and the injured and the dead being carried out by the survivors.

When the lights came on and we were sitting there, I couldn't look at anyone. I felt as if I had been kicked in the stomach, and deservedly. While I may not be in Washington giving orders, I am an American and this is what my country is doing, and here it is even clearer to me than it was in the United States. I am as guilty as Johnson, Rusk, McNamara, the Pentagon, and all the forces that are perpetuating this horror.

We have met a young Englishman, writing for the *Economist*. He has just been in Saigon and Da Nang and found the situation very depressing. He suggested that the United States needed a more "sophisticated" attitude toward the war and should be prepared for a long struggle, five or ten years. How many Americans would be willing to do this? How many have any conception of what this war is about? Adlai Stevenson said, "Let's talk sense to the American people,"—let's also talk truth and reality and then see what the statistics are about fighting a war on someone else's land 10,000 miles away and having our young men die before they have lived for a cause that no one understands.

Harrison has been trying to get to the frontier to see for himself the areas the Cambodians have accused us of shelling and bombing, which the U. S. government has denied. One trip will take several days and will be too rugged for me but I can go on a short trip to the border near Svey Rieng. We go tomorrow at 6 a.m.

June 5

TODAY I have been recovering from our "short" trip to the frontier. Svey Rieng is in the opposite direction from Angkor and some of the country seemed drier than what we have seen, though there were rice paddies all along. But there were many citrus and banana trees and long stretches of lotus plants, the beautiful pink flowers reaching up straight and high from their enormous leaves. Along the highway a lovely pale lilac flower grows, low and the foliage full. It has no smell. Many of the flowers in Cambodia are familiar; hibiscus, oleander, bougainvillea, but there are also many I don't recognize, usually with thick strong leaves and small, delicate, fragile-appearing blossoms. Something I had not seen before were boys, about ten or so, between shafts pulling large drums and cans of water. They are very heavy and it is not nice to see a young boy pulling such a load with the sweat pouring off him.

There was not much motorized traffic on the road, only a few cars and an occasional truck transporting bottled drinks; some Cambodian, some Chinese but mostly American, Pepsi Cola and Seven Up. But the road was full of people, children walking or bicycling to school, men and women going to work, driving oxen with carts carrying logs and bundles of twigs, and a few carts pulled by the pretty little horses, though these are being replaced gradually by motor bikes and trucks. Many small scrawny mongrel dogs lay in and beside the road—frightening creatures looking as if they were starving to death.

After a brief stop at Svey Rieng where we met the Governor, we set out in a command car to see some of the frontier. The Governor and Deputy Governor and several members of the local government accompanied us and our car was led and followed by officers and soldiers in jeeps. The Deputy Governor is Madame Chien-Chin Bano, pretty and very young. Most of the Cambodians we have met are very young and I keep feeling not only too big, but ancient, too. Our hosts sat on benches in the back and H. and I sat in front, I next to the driver. He coughed all the time and I wondered if he had t.b.; then I thought maybe I was giving him an allergy.

We stopped first at an outpost near the frontier and saw damage done by American bombs, and holes in the roof of a barracks made by American bullets. We saw a bomb with "made in U. S. A." on it and more in the jungle where they had fallen. Fortunately no people had been killed here, only some cows, but this was not always the case. We went next to the river, no larger than the Housatonic, and there we saw the scorching and holes made by bullets and shelling on trees, and large piles of shrapnel—sharp, twisted, lethal pieces of metal. I thought, how wicked to fire such things at people, or anything alive. What an insane way to try and solve political problems, or any problems. South Vietnam was on the other side of the river and I looked across and felt sick. Of course we shoot across the border and our bombs fall on this tiny country which is struggling for its life and doesn't want to get involved. It is too close, it can't be helped; but that doesn't justify such brutality.

A young man showed us the trenches on the banks of the river—pitiful defense against modern mechanized warfare —and demonstrated how he had shot back with a rifle at the firing from across the river. All day we drove or walked, through the jungle, over the small clearings, through the villages, all along the South Vietnamese border. I felt more and more the uselessness of this struggle, the revolting role we are playing, the incongruity of Americans in the jungle. An Australian we met here told me that there was a high death toll of Americans as much because we are not adapted to and trained for jungle fighting as from the enemy. How do the American people justify this? How does the Pentagon, Johnson, Rusk, all of them?

In the middle of the day we stopped to eat at a "maison pour repos"—a platform built out over a river with a high roof of woven leaves and open on four sides. Lunch was a picnic, our hosts said, and was served at a long table spread with a white cloth and strewn with flowers. Several pretty women, the wives of army officers in our party, had arranged the lunch and there were many helpers to wait on us. All the inhabitants for miles around gathered outside the house and watched and I wondered how we appeared to them. There was nothing rude or prying about their watching; I felt only friendly curiosity and interest.

The picnic menu included barbecued pig (their favorite part is the hide, the leather, which was like eating a football), omelette with onions, rice, soup with meat and vegetables, duck and French-fried potatoes, beefsteak, macaroni with tomato sauce, several dishes of cabbage and bean sprouts, sliced cucumbers and eggplant, platters of fresh fruit and a never-ending supply of French bread. Every place we have eaten in Cambodia the bread is superb and I keep promising myself to make bread regularly when we get home and not settle for the tasteless stuff we buy. On the table were bottles of Maggi flavoring which they use with everything. I was grateful for its strong taste with some of the dishes. It is amazing how much these people eat, and in this heat, and extraordinary that I haven't seen one fat person since we got here.

After our picnic lunch we resumed our tour of the border. The heat was almost unbearable and we stopped often for refreshing drinks of Pepsi Cola and Seven Up which had been kept cool in a huge tub of ice in the back of our car. At every stop the people collected around us asking and answering questions. Everyone was friendly and interested and seemed comforted by the fact we had come to see for ourselves what has happened.

As it began to get dark we headed back to Svey Rieng for a long three-hour, very bumpy ride. At first we were all talkative, stimulated by what we had seen and heard, but gradually talk ceased and we were nearly asleep when we arrived. The Governor's house was a blaze of lights and festoons of colored lights hung from the trees and in the gardens. We stumbled out of the car and were about to say goodby when our guide said, "You can take a shower now and then we will have a dinner." There certainly was no choice, and I suppose we should have realized that no matter what we had done all day, a formal dinner was the correct ending. We had brought nothing but the clothes we had on and after eight hours in the jungle, climbing in and out of the Land Rover, we were dirty and grimy and disheveled.

We were taken to a room off the reception hall which had an air conditioner and two beds. Across a little hall was a yellow and black tiled bathroom with every fixture that has been invented and the shower arrangement that you just stand under in the middle of the room with the water going all over—no curtain. One of those pretty filigreed silver bowls was in the basin and there were lemon soap, towels, cologne, toothbrush, toothpaste, hairbrush and comb but no water. However, the shower had water. We washed, lay down on the beds for a few minutes, put our dirty clothes back on and went to dinner.

The Governor's wife greeted us. She is having her tenth baby soon, already has seven boys and two girls. She has great poise, a very self-assured and charming hostess. I suppose she is about thirty, if that. She wore a black silk sampot and a white embroidered top and had some fine rubies. Everyone had changed and looked cool and refreshed. Their way of dressing is very becoming to women. I think we are crazy to change our fashions so often; the classic wrapping and draping is almost always more becoming than what we wear.

The dining room was separated from the reception room only by filmy white curtains which were blowing gently from the fans on the ceiling. Again the table was strewn with flowers and the dinner was elegant and elegantly served. Everything is done with great style here. All during dinner and until we left we heard the American bombing and shelling. We were only nine kms. from the border. Usually it was faint but occasionally I felt the vibration and the glasses rattled. A savage touch to this stylish, civilized evening.

After a cool drive of over two hours we got back to our hotel here at 2 a.m. It was a long, tiring day but interesting, fascinating and rewarding. I have never met people anywhere who are so friendly, hospitable and kind as the Cambodians are to us. I am surprised they are able to regard us as friends. Before we started on this trip I thought all the time about Vietnam but I didn't think much about the neighboring countries. They were unfamiliar, just names on the map. But here we are, in a country where the people feel threatened every hour, caught in the middle of forces they have no control over, trying to keep out of war, trying to live their lives in their own way, and I understand so well what they mean. When our shells land on their villages, when the war we are fighting across the river interrupts their trade and upsets their economy, their families, their lives, why should they think of us as friends?

June 6

HARRISON got word that we cannot get visas for North Vietnam at this time, so we are resuming our trip and go to Bangkok tomorrow. It is a disappointment as we had allowed ourselves to feel there was a big chance of our getting there. However, if anything does come through later we can come back from wherever we are. I am grateful for the visit we have had here and for the opportunities of seeing this lovely country and meeting and talking to so many different people. Everybody talks about the same subjects—Vietnam, China, the U. S., Cambodia's borders and her position in this dangerous and constantly shifting world. I feel, as I have felt since I began being aware of Vietnam, and more since we started on this trip, that there is just one thing that matters; this war must stop; this slaughter must cease; it is the only thing that counts. All other problems fade into nothing compared to it.

The other night at dinner with someone from the Australian Embassy, we discussed the Americans in Phnom Penh, before diplomatic relations were broken. Everyone agreed that our whole operation was too big; too many people who rented too many houses; too many cars, too much money. When they all left the cost of rents collapsed; there were so many apartments and houses vacated suddenly the owners were begging the remaining tenants to stay at very reduced rates. Why do we do things like this? Why are we so insensitive to other countries and other people? Why do we barge in like bulldozers and tanks and take over just with sheer size? Will we ever learn that old, old truth about quality vs. quantity? I am so depressed about my country and it is not because I am disloyal—in fact it is that I want so terribly to be proud of it that I feel so disappointed and also shocked, annoyed and enraged.

I am depressed about my own country and the role we are in out here, and also about this beautiful little country we are leaving. It is like a songbird surrounded by hawks, not knowing which way to turn. Vietnam on one side, China threatening, Thailand, Laos, and the U. S. Air Force much too close for comfort.

☙ *three*

June 9, Oriental Hotel, Bangkok, Thailand

WE FLEW here two days ago on a Vietnam Airline plane. The stewardesses are Vietnamese and wear white trousers and bright blue oudai, the long coats open at the sides. The girls are even prettier than the Cambodian women, with the same delicacy and style.

While I have known that we have a certain amount of army in Thailand, I wasn't prepared for the long rows of American Air Force planes lined up at the airport here or the vast numbers of American service men everywhere I go, some who seem to be on active duty, some travelling through, and many in large groups on leave from fighting in Vietnam.

From the air Thailand looks like Cambodia, though the

colors seem to be a little duller, a sort of gray tone over all, and everything on a slightly bigger scale. But as we landed and came into the city we sensed the difference at every turn. Here there is a confusion and bustling not strictly oriental. It is more like Hong Kong at first glance; men in business suits or casual sport clothes; others in their native-type trousers, and always the U. S. uniforms. The women's native dress is a long skirt similar to the Cambodian's sampot and many wear this or long black trousers, especially the older women. But others wear short slit skirts or Western clothes. Most women seem to have short hair as compared to the long luxurious braids of the Cambodians. And there are tourists even though this is the off season. But I don't feel either the sophisticated worldly flavor of Hong Kong or the beautiful natural rhythm of Cambodia; perhaps there hasn't been time for the differences to blend. It is oriental with a heavy coating of involvement with the U. S. war in Vietnam—a strange mixture. In fact, it doesn't mix very well—it is like a heavy frame on a small picture or too much thick gravy on a delicate piece of meat. Here a lot of English is spoken and I don't feel as oversized as I did in Cambodia because the people seem bigger and some are even plump. But heavens, the white visitors are fat—French, German, American—some really grotesque.

Bangkok is a burgeoning city with many of the problems of our cities; too much expansion and growth without enough planning. Pedicabs, trolley cars, taxis, buses, bicycles, automobiles, trucks—every kind of vehicle—pushing through streets not designed for so much traffic; air pollution from too many exhausts and industrial chimneys; noise. There is a tension and nervousness in the atmosphere as if life has taken on an unnatural urgency and there isn't time to work out anything properly.

Our hotel is the only hotel on the river and from our window we have a wonderful view. This is like Hong Kong, like the harbor there. At intervals on the water large freighters roll at their anchors; barges covered with corrugated metal roofs looking like floating Quonset huts carry great loads of fruit, vegetables, lumber and other commodities; fringed-top launches take sightseers on excursion trips and everyday passengers going about their business; a few pull barges. Small boats remind me of the smallest sampan taxis in Aberdeen harbor of Hong Kong. Men or women, but mostly women, propel these boats directly across the river from one side to the other in spite of the strong current. As everyone who has seen them has mentioned, they swing one leg gracefully as they work the long oar.

There are elevators at opposite ends of the hall downstairs and to get to our room from one elevator we get off on the fourth floor and from the other we get off on the fifth and land in the same place. There are several bellboys bossed by an elderly Chinese man and they all come into our room whenever they feel like it; if the door is locked they open it with a key. There is a bolt inside but we keep forgetting to use it.

This morning I visited the Palace and the Temple of the Emerald Bhudda and the surrounding buildings. It is a fairyland of color and delicacy—truly gorgeous. So much gold, so much color, so much decoration. If there is an inch undecorated it is solid gold. It is more lavish than the palace at Phnom Penh. Also went to Wat Po which is a work-a-day temple with people selling souvenirs, living in corners. I saw a woman drying rice on six large mats and family wash hanging on a line. A house of corrugated tin was in a corner behind a small temple—it seemed like a sort of camp ground.

We lunched at the Bann Thai restaurant with a friend of Harrison's in the Thailand Foreign Office. They met in Moscow in 1953 and used to play poker together and haven't seen each other since. There were a few low tables where guests sat on the floor, but we sat on chairs at a conventional (for us) table. We each had a large covered bowl of rice and five smaller bowls filled with delectable concoctions of shrimp, chicken, noodles, bean sprouts, crab, and many unknown substances. Food is terribly hot here. Our dessert was fruit, arranged on a small curved plate and decorated with flowers and buds carved out of white, white potatoes, whiter than any white I ever saw, stuck onto green stems and leaves. It reminded me of carving things out of ivory soap when we were children but our results were never like this. We didn't talk about Vietnam and I was relieved. It is such a heavy burden all the time and even if I can never forget it, it is a relief not to be always talking about it.

In the afternoon I took a launch up the river to Wat Arun. It is so different from the temples at Angkor, very high, much more compact, and all decorated with color. From a distance it looks like mosaic; close to, you see that it is all done with chips and pieces of china and pottery stuck in cement—a fantastic idea. I would think the result would be clumsy but the effect is dainty and fragile. The sun went down very suddenly on the way back and it was much cooler and actually refreshing on the water.

June 10

Tʜɪs morning I went to see Mr. J. Thompson's house. He is the American who came here to live after World War II and started the famous silk business that is now known all over the world. He has done a lot for the industry and, besides his shop, has factories and many people working for him. His house is made up of several real Thai houses, moved from different places and put together in the most attractive way. There are thick, green jungly plants and ferns planted in the many courtyards among the buildings which are all connected inside and filled with treasures from Cambodia, Thailand, Burma and China. It is situated on the edge of a klong, one of the canals running all through Bangkok, and directly across are some of the houses where the silk is woven and dyed. Brilliant turquoise and wild pink silk hung in lengths out over the water and I could see inside the buildings where women sat winding thread.

Tomorrow morning early H. and I are going to take a boat trip through the klongs and see the famous floating markets. He hasn't been able to do much sightseeing and I have done most of mine alone or with a friend I have made, a young American man who has survived two years in Vietnam and is now out of the Army and batting around because he feels so unsettled, and doesn't know where to turn, where to go, or what to do. I imagine war does that to many boys. It must shake up everything, values and thoughts, so it might even be impossible to settle down to anything. He said that what the Australian in Cambodia told us is true; that Americans have many fatalities not inflicted by the enemy but caused by ignorance and lack of training and discipline. He said, for instance, that sometimes after a group of Americans was surprised by the Vietcong and had to hide quickly, duck into holes, etc., as soon as the immediate shooting was over, the soldiers would pop up to see what was happening, or light a cigarette, or even take a picture, and, of course, would be shot. This also fits into something else we have been told; that the soldiers who do survive the first few jungle battles learn fast how to protect themselves and turn into tough fighters.

June 11

EARLY this morning H. and I took our boat ride down the river and through the klongs, through the floating markets and back to the hotel. The network of klongs is vast and a lot of the life of Bangkok is lived on and beside and in them. Many are being filled in to make roads, which is a pity. Houses are on posts out and over the water and everyone was washing—either the dishes, clothes, babies and children, themselves; having a very soapy shampoo, or sometimes just scrubbing off the steps leading from the house into the water. I imagine they get pretty slimy unless scrubbed often. We noticed many boxes of FAB detergent.

The klong was not very wide and there were many traffic jams and near collisions. The sight-seeing boats are usually the fringed-top flattish boats that must hold twenty or more passengers comfortably. We had one to ourselves with a man at the helm and a boy to fend off other boats and help at landings, etc., and there were four boats just like ours ahead of us. The klong taxis are long and narrow with tiny propellers at the end of a long spear-like engine—they look like small sharks darting dangerously through the melee, sounding a sharp horn. The markets are the small boats usually propelled by a woman, and laden down with food —all kinds of vegetables, fish in every state, fresh, fried, dried; coconuts, fruits. Some had loads of charcoal; these boats were bigger and propelled by a man and a woman, both appropriately dressed in black. Here many women had short hair, as in the city streets. The life in the houses is as active as the life on the klong and many people were in the water, to get from one place to the other and children swimming just for fun. How they escape the taxi propellers or being run down by boats is a miracle.

When we came back I had my hair done in the hotel. In the beauty parlors in Cambodia I leaned back in a chair and my hair was washed in a long trough with faucets and sprays at intervals. Several heads could have been washed at the same time and I wondered if the dirty soap and water got all mixed up. Five girls assisted there, with combing, curling, pinning, doing the coiffure, and a small electric fan blew gently on me all the time to relieve the heat. Here, I lay down on a slightly slanting sort of stretcher bed and had a very thorough shampoo. The girl scrubbed and scrubbed and kept turning my head gently from side to side so she could get at the back. I felt I had no control—she moved me as if I were paralyzed or dead and it went through my mind that it was as if she were washing the hair on a corpse. But it was comfortable and, as I said, thorough. Only two women helped roll and curl and then comb it out, not five.

Late this afternoon we are going to Burma. General Ne Win sent us a personal invitation to visit his country. We do not know why exactly but I suppose it is because of his trip to the U. S., planned for September. Perhaps he thinks the *New York Times* will give him good publicity if he lets one of their men into his country. He could use some good press; his treatment of U Nu doesn't endear him to many Americans. Though our actions towards unsympathetic systems of government in other countries are aggressive and punitive, at least in our own country we still vote people in and out of office; we don't put them in jail. This is another coup for Harrison. No American journalist has been to Burma recently and while we do have an ambassador and other government agencies in Rangoon, Burma has closed her doors to foreign business and travellers in her effort to take the business and economy out of the hands of and control by foreigners, mainly the Indians and the Chinese.

I wish we could stay here a little longer. I would like to get out into the country to see if there I would feel the way I do about this city. What is sort of awful and shocking is that the Thais are making money out of their connection with us and the war in Vietnam. American money is pouring into their country and many people are getting rich. What is the morality of this? I guess it just means that people always make money out of war. Some say that is why this war won't end for years; too many people are profiting from it.

 *four*

June 14, Rangoon, Strand Hotel

WE LEFT Bangkok Saturday afternoon late in a
Burmese Airline plane which had been sent especially from
here to pick up an American doctor, his wife and two children and us. He is the new doctor attached to the U. S.
Embassy. We were the only passengers. Most of the flight
was over thick green jungle and when we landed at Rangoon it was dark.

This hotel is wonderful—a big old colonial type where I
expect to meet some romantic character from the past at
each turn. Downstairs is a big entrance hall with floor of
black and white marble squares; the ceiling above it goes up
to the roof and rooms are on two floors around the wide
stair-well. Tables and chairs are in the hall and you can have
drinks there instead of in the bar. There is one regular din-

ing room, a large room for receptions, a bar, a writing room, a barber shop. Where there isn't marble the floors are teak, beautifully laid and polished. Around and off the hall are several offices for travel agencies and services related to tourists but these are all empty, the doors are locked and we can just look through the wide windows and imagine the pictures and maps that used to be displayed to tempt the guests who formerly filled this hotel. Although we usually use the elevator because the boy is always standing hopefully beside it and we can't bear to disappoint him, we occasionally sneak to the staircase, which is curved and grand —appropriate for kings and generals and beautiful women to sweep up and down.

Our room is huge and has very high ceilings, two ceiling fans and an air conditioner. There are two wide beds, a dressing table, desk, sofa and two armchairs; several tables and lots of space. The ceilings must be twenty feet high. The service is excellent and all the people are nice and friendly but, oh dear, it is depressing. As there are no tourists there are hardly any guests here, just us and a group of five Eastern European business men, and I believe the hotel could hold two hundred or more. At meals in the dining room there are usually more waiters than guests, though in the evening there are a few regular diners from the outside. The manager is the former owner-manager but now the government has taken it over. It is curious they keep such a large staff and I wonder if they are perhaps going to change their policy about tourists. I should think Burma could use some tourist money—it might pep up their general level of life.

The city seems dead; many buildings are empty, shut and boarded up; all the foreign libraries are closed. There is no student exchange and the only foreign programs, aid or otherwise, are those which were started before 1963. There are very few shops and these are sad sights indeed. A lacquer store which was renowned for its wares a few years ago was shabby and dirty and the few pieces of lacquer for sale were covered with dust in a glass showcase which must not have been opened for many months. I visited a jeweler who showed his obvious embarrassment at having nothing to offer except inferior jade instead of the rubies and emeralds he formerly dealt in. The government owns the mines now. A woman who has lived here for several years took me to the big public market and I was appalled. There is really nothing to buy; what is displayed looks like goods in a second-rate Five and Ten cent store in a back country town; plastic bags and toys, cheap thin cotton shirts for children, a few little girls' dresses, Five and Ten type jewelry of plastic (not exactly what I would expect to find in an Asian country where people are famous for working with their hands with fine materials), a few straw hats, parasols, tin cooking utensils. Brooms of straw for the house or garden were the most attractive and useful objects I saw; there were no older children's clothes, no thread, no needles, no material. We are told that each individual is allowed material for one new longyi (the long wrapped skirt worn by both men and women) a year. Imagine most Americans if they could have just one skirt or one pair of trousers a year. There are plenty of the sandals everyone wears in Asia, and brassieres, which are more like a bodice and many are padded. But these were the only articles of clothing I saw.

On street corners we saw vendors with small supplies of toothpaste, soap, tiny plastic toys, strings of beads. Repairing the black umbrellas which everyone carries against rain or sun is a good sidewalk business as there are no new ones to be had.

There seems to be enough food. Baskets and wagons are loaded with fruits and vegetables and a large area of the market place is given over to the meat market. I am surprised to see so much meat in a Buddhist country. Accustomed to cold storage or frozen meats as I am, the sight of all those carcasses and insides covered with flies in this suffocating heat is repulsive.

This hotel is on the Rangoon, or Hlaing, river and it could all be so attractive. Across the street is a stretch of green—I hesitate to say park because, like everything else, it is run-down, overgrown and filled with trash—reaching down to the river. A boat station, also housing an informal restaurant, is right on the bank and usually a few people are sitting at tables eating or drinking cool drinks. A huge freighter from Bremen is anchored in the river and a few small boats dart back and forth, but not with the energy of the boats on the other harbors and rivers we have seen, Hong Kong or the Mekong or the Chao Phraya in Bangkok. I saw a boat with a full sail coming down the river very fast before the wind and it gave me an idea of how very pretty these rivers must have been when all the boats went with the wind and the current like that. There are small boats propelled by men, not women, here, and they use two oars in a backward stroke, the oars crossing each time. The boats have a turned-up bow and a split stern.

Sunday morning we went to the Shwe Dagon Pagoda, the largest and one of the oldest in the world. Up more than one hundred steps is the huge marble platform from which the gold spire rises, surrounded by hundreds of small temples of all shapes and sizes. Lots of delicate work with pieces of mirror, colored glass, wood carving and gold, gold, gold. Bazaars on the steps sell flowers, incense, candles, packages of gold leaf, for offerings; ivory and lacquer ware and pretty wood carvings were made as we watched. Two elevators, modern and monstrous, stand incongruously beside the teak-covered steps and the beautiful Burmese people were occupied making offerings, washing off the statues, praying, applying more gold to the already shining Buddhas. It reminded me of Catholic cathedrals in Italy and Spain; so much going on. And far more life up here than in the city itself. When they are not at the pagodas I wonder what the people do. There can't be enough work for everyone with so much shut down. I know they go to the movies—at any time of day there are large crowds waiting to get into the theatres—to see English, American and Asian movies. They don't show Italian movies; too sexy. I don't see where the money comes from to buy the tickets.

Last night we dined with General and Mrs. Ne Win. They called and said a car would pick us up at 6:15 for a reception at 6:30, followed by dinner. We didn't know what to expect but the reception sounded large and formal. We wondered who would be there; probably just their government people because they don't have any social communication with the embassies or the few foreigners who are here. We drove through some very well-guarded gates on the outskirts of the city (H. noticed that the whole area was dotted with patrol posts), up a winding driveway and stopped in front of a big castle-like building. (Our hostess told me later that they had a much nicer house of their own but had been living in this, really out of suitcases, for three years). A big, friendly, good-looking soldier, not a servant, met us and led us to a beautiful living room, at the end of which were two men. One jumped up, came toward us holding out his hand and said in the most friendly informal way, "I'm General Win," as if he were plain Bill Smith, an ordinary host anywhere in the world. He is very handsome and wore a light-colored longyi, white shirt and dark jacket. The other man was Brigadier Thaung Dan, Minister of Information and of Culture (most members of the government hold two or three positions). He was dressed in the same way. We sat down, had drinks and talked, just the four of us, (this turned out to be the extent of the reception) or rather just General Win and H., as the Minister said not a word the whole night and I didn't say much.

The room was a good size, a bright red carpet covering the floor and in the middle a large handsome Bokhara rug. We sat in a window seat and all around the room were many big armchairs covered with heavy beige silk. Curtains were beige and gold. A beautiful crystal chandelier hung in the middle of the ceiling. Small tables among the chairs were black and gold lacquer and were very pretty, and in the middle of the window seat was a round table made out of a large drum, heavily encrusted with gold, cut glass and stones. A Burmese harp was on a stand at the other end of the room, a graceful instrument like a curved boat, made of a sapling, leather from the breast of a doe and strings of silk held in place with cords of red braided silk.

Madame Win joined us after half an hour. She, also, is handsome and attractive with a strong, definite character which I felt instantly. She wore a dark silk longyi, a dark lace top with long sleeves and some wonderful jewelry, mostly rubies. She doesn't seem as purely Burmese and

Asian as her husband, I guess because she was educated at a convent and has many American friends. She loves New York and the Plaza Hotel. She is called Katie.

We went in to a huge state dining hall for dinner. It is all dark woodwork and looked black and menacing. But Madame has great taste and it was arranged charmingly; the table was small and in the middle and one forgot about the rest of the room. A spray of orchids was in a vase and the table set with lovely old silver in the shell pattern, and beautiful glasses. This was a feast, like so many of the dinners we have been to in Asia, but much more informal and home-like, though elegant. Four or five servants waited on us but several of the dishes were put on the table for us to serve ourselves. They have an attractive custom of Mrs. W. helping Harrison and the General helping me, but of course they gave us much too much. We had ice cream made from durian fruit, which was good and the flavor not strong at all. We were told by Milton Osborne in Cambodia that to eat the fruit was like eating strawberries and cream in a public lavatory; the taste is delicious but the smell obnoxious and foul. We had a chance to find that out this morning, which I'll describe when I finish about dinner.

We talked mainly about Burma, the problems the government is having with business, social conditions, health; the transportation and distribution of food; but most of all about their passionate desire to be free and neutral and running their own country themselves and not be beholden to any foreign government—China, India, the U. S. or anyone. They were friendly hospitable hosts and we felt honored to have been asked for such an intimate evening. Meeting all these people mixed up in these shaky governments in such unfamiliar surroundings, I am afraid of saying the wrong thing so much that I know I miss opportunities to find out more about what they think or maybe make a friend, or at least get a little closer to someone. But it is hard—we are in some ways so different, yet I haven't felt that anyone we have met so far on this trip is really different—it's just the cultural coating. But often that is impossible to break through.

As we were finishing dinner the General said he had a lot of homework to do with the Cultural Minister and they had to work at night. To be polite I said that because he was so busy they should send us home. But my politeness wasn't necessary; as we walked from the diningroom into the hall we saw that the car was waiting with two men holding the doors open for us. I thought how nice it would be if we could do that when people we have for dinner stay on and on and we want either to work or go to bed.

The other night in the dining room the head steward asked me if I had tried any of the special Burmese fruits. I said, yes, I was familiar with mangos and mangosteens and liked them a lot. Whereupon he said he would get some for me, that they don't serve mangosteens because the red color comes off on the napkins and can't be washed out, and guests don't like the smell of the durian, but that it is delicious and I should try it. The next day at lunch he reminded me that he had fruit for me, so I chose to have mangosteens. A bowl of them was brought in, with paper napkins and a fingerbowl and I ate two or three after he ceremoniously opened them for me.

We were out at the General's last night and I didn't think about the fruit until this morning when the telephone rang and it was the steward saying he had a durian for me and what were my wishes. Being full of the good breakfasts we have here I only wished he hadn't called up and that I wouldn't have to eat any more. But something happens to me with food; I make a small remark to be polite and immediately my plate is heaped to the ceiling; more new things are pressed on me; people go to all lengths to see that I have enough. I should have learned from that evening in Svey Rieng when I was just about to be sick from eating so much but managed to say I thought something was good, and Madame replied, "We don't believe you unless you ask for three helpings."

As usual I didn't know how to say no, so said I would have it now—why not? He said fine, to send our floor steward down to the kitchen. I wasn't sure what a durian looked like but had a vague idea it was small. A few minutes passed and the head steward himself arrived with a tray on which were two plates, two fingerbowls, one knife, one large spoon and the durian, which turned out to be bigger than most coconuts and all prickly on the outside. He set down the tray, opened all the windows and made sure the door to the hall was open; then he cut into the durian, which took a lot of force, and he pulled it apart. Even with the ventilation and two fans and the air conditioner, the smell was overpowering, really disgusting, and the fruit looked repulsive, soft and slimy. Thank God there wasn't too much of it as there are large seeds. He said, "You just eat it with your hands," but I couldn't bear to touch it, so ate a little with the spoon. It wasn't a bit like eating strawberries in a public lavatory; only the latter simile is true. The steward stood by anxiously waiting for my enthusiastic approval and it was pretty hard to say much. It was TER-RIBLE. Thank heaven he left and H. and I threw what we could in the toilet, messed the rest about a bit and sent for our room steward to take it away. We finally got the smell out of the room, but the hall smelt for two days. And the wretched thing cost $2.00.

June 16, Rangoon

H. SUGGESTED to General Win that we would like to see some of the country, especially Lashio and northern Burma, and the General had told Brigadier Thaung Dan to arrange a trip for us. So the Ministry of Information did just that; they sent us on a guided tour of Mandalay and Pagan, the two best-known attractions in Burma but not one inch into the north or anywhere else. It amuses me that nothing was said about Lashio; we were simply taken just where they wanted us to go and saw only what they wanted us to see. Why we weren't allowed to go further north we can just guess at; no facilities to take care of us, poor transportation, unrest, poverty, fighting among the tribes, who knows. But we had a most interesting trip and are grateful for the opportunity to see what we did.

Mandalay is a romantic word and conjures up memories of my father singing Kipling's famous song and my young girl's dreams of handsome British soldiers pining away for the beautiful Burmese women they would love forever. Yesterday morning at 7:15 a government car picked us up and as we drove to the airport I felt nostalgic yet curious at the same time. We thought we were to take the regular commercial flight to Mandalay which goes each week, but we were taken to a special part of the airport and into the General's own private plane, a two-engine C47. Already aboard were representatives from the Foreign Office, the Ministry of Information and the Ministry of Culture, the pilot, Ernie, a charming, talkative man who took some of his training in Alabama and Colorado, and the second pilot. The flight took about two hours and we flew so low we could see first miles of rice paddies, then thick, thick forests, then civilization again and Mandalay. The Irrawaddy river is enormous and water seems to be spread out over the land far from its banks. Hundreds of white pagodas are dotted about and two of the most famous, the gold Eindawaya and the Kaunghmudaw, shaped like a full breast, are especially conspicuous. The chief officer of the army in Mandalay met us and accompanied us to the guest house, built by the British, in a military compound, where we were to spend the night. Our room was upstairs and occupied most of the space over the two rooms below. In it were six beds and three air conditioners. A sign with an arrow saying "toilet room" pointed out one door and down a corridor; adjacent was a shower stall and next to that a basin with a mirror above. We settled ourselves, had a cool drink with our entourage, plus the new officers who were to be with us in Mandalay, and started off—three carloads full.

Our first stop was at a music school. Girls and boys are trained here in the traditional music and dances which seem to us so much like the Cambodian and Thai dances, but to an expert are very different. The children entertained us with several dances and songs accompanied by drums, cymbals and the Burmese harp. The drums were large, lavishly decorated gold drums the same as the table in General Win's living room. The performances were excellent and professional though some of the children were tiny. We sat with the headmaster and the teachers sat around the edge of the room looking very proud.

We next visited the site of the palace which is inside the high red brick walls of the old city. These have been destroyed many times in many places but are being restored. The palace itself, along with most of its immediate walls and all but a few remnants of three smaller outbuildings, was destroyed in World War II. The Japanese were inside and held out until the Allies had shelled it to powder. To see such destruction and to realize it was done only twenty years ago, and by us and the British, no matter who caused it, is a shock. It seems reasonable to see ruins from the past, but ruins of the present are something else. Who are the beasts here so close to the jungle? The animals or the humans?

The government is reconstructing the palace and it will be a museum. Unfortunately, they have put in posts made of cement instead of teak, as they were in the original. Perhaps the cement can be painted to resemble wood, but it seems too bad to cut corners this way. This country is so poor financially and has cut itself off from any foreign exchange and trade. It is trying so hard to keep going on its own and be independent; their pride is touching and sad. Everything I see here is broken down or worn out and seedy, and I am reminded of my father's Bostonian friend, Harry Shattuck. Looking up at the peeling, flaking ceiling in the kitchen of our Cape Cod summer house he said, "This is what I like—shabby." But I think even he and my father would think the shabbiness here not the kind they liked.

When we returned to the house for lunch we found all the beds but two had been taken out of our room; soft toilet paper replaced the harsh roll that had been there before;

Lux soap was on the basin and in the shower. After a seven-course lunch, which we are getting used to, and a short rest, we spent the afternoon on a tour of Mandalay's pagodas. It was a whirlwind tour and we drove so fast from place to place it was hard to keep up with where we were. It is surprising that in all this heat people eat so much and move so fast. The Burmese are like the Cambodians in these respects. They never seem to get tired and yet with all the constant movement there is none of the feverish tension of the West. It all seems perfectly natural.

On the whole I didn't find Mandalay's pagodas very attractive or appealing. They are so congested, so many small pagodas, steps, shops, people living all over, so much dirt. And I don't like all the whitewash except from the air. But we didn't feel as depressed as we have in Rangoon. There seemed to be more cheerful normal life going on; more goods in the stores, more things for sale. There are lots of those pretty little horses pulling carts full of people or wood and food or both. And many bicycles, but there are lots of these in Rangoon, too. We see more pregnant women in Burma than in either Cambodia or Thailand but fewer children. Strange.

Early this morning we flew from Mandalay to Pagan. Pagan is Burma's Angkor. At its height, before the Mongols swept through and destroyed the city, there were over 5,000 temples. Only about five hundred remain, in varying states of decay. The countryside is like our West, parts of Arizona, Colorado and Utah. The earth is red and it is very dry in spite of the huge river and this being the monsoon period. It is a flat plain surrounded by hills and covered with rough grasses and a few low scrubby trees. We climbed the highest platform on one of the temples and we could see towers and remains of many temples stretching out on all sides. Most were built originally of brick and a few of sandstone. I love the brick. It is just the same color as the earth and the temples seem to grow right up out of the red dirt. The gray-white of the sandstone appears more delicate. They say that the sandstone was cut in large blocks from the hill several miles away and handed from man to man from the hill to the site of the temple being built. The temples still being used for worship (and also those in which the colors have worn away and the frescoes spoiled) are whitewashed and these, like the pagodas in Rangoon, are surrounded by many small pagodas and steps covered with a succession of carved teak roofs. Here and there we saw corrugated tin on a roof, which seems out of place when you think of it but not when you look at it; anything goes in a Burmese pagoda, it seems. There isn't the mystery of Angkor in Pagan, probably because it is flat open country and you can see everything at once, while at Angkor fantastic things appear suddenly out of the jungle growth and take you by surprise.

As in Angkor, the government is rebuilding and restoring as much as they can. But it is a long expensive process and here again, it would be such a help to have some of the money tourists are dying to spend.

In another guest house built by the British we had lunch; ten courses and the famous Mandalay beer, good if hot. We flew back here in a monsoon thunderstorm which came suddenly, terrifyingly.

Tomorrow we leave for New Delhi. Still no word about North Vietnam. In some ways I am relieved, in others disappointed. Here I have gotten a little away from the constant pressure due to the war. The Burmese have so many problems of their own that we have talked more about them than about our war. But in no conversation has the subject of Vietnam been omitted; it is just not always first and foremost in people's minds the way it is in Cambodia.

We have had a lovely visit and have been captivated by all the people we have met. The Burmese are friendly, charming, attractive, with warmth and humor, and just about all of them, men and women, are beautiful.

≋ *five*

June 17, On plane to Calcutta

THERE is not one empty seat on this plane and all
the passengers except us are Indians. They are leaving
Burma, some after generations, because they can't have
their own businesses any more under the present govern-
ment-controlled Burmese system. We understand that many
of the Chinese, who owned most of what the Indians did
not, have chosen to remain and will work in their former
businesses for the Burmese government. This is something
to think about; even though they may not be sympathetic
to Peking at the moment their loyalty is probably first to
China under any circumstances, and here they are and here
they will be when and if they might be necessary to Peking.
But the Indians do not choose to do this. They are returning

to India to start life again—refugees—as so many people have been and are in our modern world.

I don't imagine most groups of refugees look so colorful. The women are wearing beautiful saris of beautiful colors, blue, deep pink, orange, red, and lots and lots of jewelry. Most of the men have turbans or white Gandhi hats, and some are in regular Western suits and others in the white Indian dhoti. We are jammed into a DC6 and many passengers are sick; those not throwing up are coughing and sneezing. The stewardess has on a brown and gold sari and looks as if she were going to the opera or to dinner with a king. She passes out paper bags and tends to all the grubbiness like a beautiful Indian Florence Nightingale dressed by an Asian Dior. Strangely, she has a gold cross around her neck. The lady in front of us is dressed in a silver brocade blouse, a gorgeous blue sari embroidered with silver, many jewels—earrings, bracelets, rings; more in her hair and a diamond in her nose. She is having a terrible time. She has been sick most of the way and her husband constantly fans her. Her lunch is still on her lap; she must have hopes of feeling improved, but if the lunch looks to her the way it did to me, she will be sick again.

Dum Dum Airport, Calcutta, Waiting for the plane to New Delhi

Our neighbor lady made quite a good recovery for a while but then had a relapse. Her husband resumed his fanning but by this time their little girl was crying. Poor man—comforting his child and fanning his beautifully dressed, vomiting wife. I am glad we couldn't see any other passengers; hearing them was enough and the ventilation being what it was, I was glad to get here.

June 21, New Delhi

THE trip from Calcutta to Delhi was very different from the trip from Rangoon. Our plane was a sleek Viscount, not too big, and only two seats on each side of the aisle. The stewardesses were lovely and wore the same brown and gold saris as the girl in the Rangoon plane, but they were far more casual. One was extremely pretty and from a distance looked like Ellen, which I remarked to H. When she came near us we were nearly blinded by her eye make-up and Harrison said, "A combination of Ellie and Theda Bara." The flight was from six to nine forty and we hoped for something to eat that we *could* eat (I had had nothing since breakfast) but the time went by and the only sign of food were several trays that went up to the captain and crew. Finally the stewardess who reminded us of Ellen walked slowly through the plane handing out paper napkins and I was sure that meant food, until we noticed she didn't give one to every passenger, just here and there, and only one to me, not Harrison. We discovered they were to wipe off the drops of water falling on the passenger nearest the window from the ventilators which were open. The air coming in was so cold the moisture had frozen, then began melting and dripping. So we wiped off the side of the airplane and sat back—hungry for the first time on this trip.

Eventually they brought us some dinner and the chicken was good.

We are staying at Roosevelt House as guests of Ambassador and Mrs. Bowles. This is the official United States residence for our ambassador but the Bowles' prefer to live in the house they lived in when they were here before when he was ambassador under President Truman. At first I was surprised at this, but now that we have lived in Roosevelt House for a few days and have seen their house, I understand it perfectly.

The United States Embassy and Roosevelt House were designed by Edward Stone and every American can be proud of the way they look. Close to each other yet separated by high white walls and wonderful planting of flowering trees and shrubs, they are a triumph of taste and beauty. The Embassy is especially beautiful with a huge round fountain in the driveway and wide high marble steps leading up to the door. Inside, the offices open off a court which has a long pool with the cooling sound of dripping water and plants and flowers in and around it. We are told that the enormous American staff here has already outgrown the space and additional offices have been built.

Roosevelt House is also beautiful with high glass doors opening onto porches all around and much filigree work. Both buildings are white which is prettier and cooler than colors. Roosevelt House is furnished and decorated with attractive furniture and appropriate and lovely rugs and fabrics. Pictures by contemporary American artists are on loan from the Museum of Modern Art in New York, the Phillips Gallery in Washington, and private collections, and hang in most of the rooms. Looking at these two govern-

Volunteers we have met; they are simple and natural and dignified and proud of what they are doing. Narish tells us they are much appreciated; they live the way the villagers do and are completely separate from anything political.

Outside of one village was a gypsy camp, but it was not like the pictures in old storybooks. I have never seen such filth. There were no beautiful, romantic gypsies, only tragic, furtive women, dressed in rags and covered with hammered-out silver jewelry. One old hag wearing glasses and a ring in her nose squatted in a doorway, but most of the adults hid their faces and seemed troubled by us. The children were friendly and curious and looked healthy and happy. Several little ones were playing with manure in a shallow water hole, making mud pies with it.

In all the villages and at intervals along the roads are wells. Some are new with pipes and faucets and separate places for washing and drinking; some are old and a container is lowered and water pulled up. Women, and often young children, carry the water on their heads in gleaming metal jugs. A firm ring fits onto their heads and the jug rests on that. In one village we got a glimpse of a butcher shop as we walked by. It was too repulsive to describe—worse than any so far—people squatting on tables amidst the raw meat, and flies all over everything. It is so hot and there are so many flies, I long for a real ice cold wind to blow it all away—not air conditioning cold; real, winter cold.

Before we went to see the Taj Mahal we drove through Agra to Fatehpur Sikri. This city was built by Akbar in the years 1569–74 and abandoned about fifty years later because of the poor supply of water. Abandoned cities were usually ransacked and pillaged and there was very little left, but this is practically intact. There doesn't seem to be any special reason for this condition; it is spooky and eerie—as if time had stopped. I expected the king and members of the court to emerge from the buildings any minute. The king had a bedroom ideal for this climate. There were windows in the thick walls, narrow and high, to let in air but not sun; his bed was high off the floor, he had to climb up stone steps to get onto it, and the floor was a pool of rose water. It got awfully hot while we were walking around; there is nothing but stone, no trees or grass or gardens and of course, no rose water.

Then we went to Agra. We parked outside, went up and through the gate and my immediate reaction was the same as everyone else's who has seen the Taj Mahal in all these centuries—simply that it is the most beautiful thing I have ever seen. It wasn't a surprise the way Venice was, which far surpassed anything I had dreamed of. I had no expectations about the Taj Mahal, in fact I had a sort of un-expecting feeling. And then it was just there, just a fact, this sheer, pure beauty, the most beautiful creation in the world. It has been ever since it was built and it always will be. It is as simple as that. But you have to be there to realize it. Perfection cannot be described or photographed or painted, or in any way reproduced. It can only be seen and felt; it goes directly to you.

It was terribly hot and even H. minded it and suggested getting under my umbrella. We had a picnic lunch in the back of a shop owned by friends of our driver and cooled by air conditioning and fans, and started home afterwards. It was too hot to go through the fort; we drove to it, looked longingly but didn't have the strength to get out of the car. Some day I would like to come here in the fall and winter when it is cooler, and have the energy to really see the sights of old India and be able to take time to go back the next day to something especially appealing, which almost everything is.

I don't accompany Harrison when he talks to diplomats and government people but the other afternoon I went along with him to visit the Family Planning Center. He interviewed the head, an ex-army colonel doctor, and we heard about the program and how they are trying to cope with the frightening population explosion here. The Colonel fiddled and toyed with a loop all the time he was talking to us and once reached over, handed it to me and asked, "Have you had any experience with the loop, Mrs. Salisbury?" He showed us a box which looked like a camera case, which contained a model of female anatomy. The nurse or social worker takes it around and shows the women what their bodies are like, how they work, how the loop fits into the picture, or rather, into them, and how it is inserted. H. said afterwards he wouldn't think the model would go over very easily with uneducated people and I agree with him; those things always make me feel uncomfortable. But I imagine that if I were one of the women I have seen in the villages, having my first baby while still in my teens and another every year until I couldn't have any more or my poor body gave out from starvation, disease, or sheer exhaustion, I would be willing to try anything to prevent pregnancy if it were explained in a kind and sympathetic way. There can't be any joy in women's lives when they have to live like this; none of the excitement of having a baby, none of the curiosity as to whether a girl or boy, light hair or dark, blue eyes or brown; none of the wonder, when you first hold your baby after his birth, at this miracle in your arms. It must be just another mouth to feed, another stomach to fill, another child to bring up, or watch suffer and die under conditions no human being should have to live under. It does seem to go over, and it is certainly good for women to know just what is happening, and how and where. There are big billboards around the city with a picture of an Indian woman doctor showing a loop to an Indian woman. The caption reads, "Loop for family planning,"—some in Hindi, some in English. Often they are alongside very sexy ads for Indian movies. A young man told me a popular motto is, "Loop before you leap."

Along with many other people we have met here, we have enjoyed seeing the Bowles'. They are so simple and direct, so unflashy and sincere, and so dedicated to India and their job out here. It is wonderful to feel the way I do about them—proud and somehow better about my country than I have been feeling—not so frustrated and depressed. Mrs. Bowles wears a sari a lot of the time and when I first heard this I didn't understand it, even thought it was a little affected. Now I see how sensible it is, and how polite of her. A sari is the ideal dress for this climate; it is loose and cool, requires few underclothes, protects one from the wind, the dust, the bugs, the sun, and the end piece can cover the head if one wishes or hang softly over the shoulder. There is no sewing involved, just six yards of material wrapped correctly. I realize, also, that most Indians are flattered that an Ambassador's wife wears their native style. It generates the same sort of feeling that learning their language creates.

We have not dwelt on the problem of Vietnam all the time but have had many pleasant conversations about life and politics in Connecticut, sailing on Long Island Sound, our families and mutual friends. It is a comfort to talk of normal things even though, as in Burma, the talk comes

70

around in the end, inevitably, to Vietnam. While India may not mind having the United States Army between her and China, I haven't heard any Indian, man or woman, say anything except that they deplore the war and wish it would stop. Everyone seems to feel that there is something abhorrent about a big, huge industrial power like the United States moving in on a little peasant country—spreading out over the rice paddies, through the jungles into the tiny villages, with bulldozers, cranes, steam rollers, tanks—all the enormous machines of our technological culture. It is so incongruous and out of place—too big for the surroundings, as we seem in contrast to the smaller, daintier people of Southeast Asia. A bull in a china shop certainly seems apropos.

Tomorrow we are going to Sikkim to visit the Queen. Though she went to college with Ellen, she was a year ahead, and I never happened to meet her when I visited Sarah Lawrence. We fly at six a.m. back to Calcutta, then take another plane straight north to Bagdogra. From there we shall see. There have been heavy rains and floods recently and Sikkim was cut off from the rest of the world for several days. But we are assured that everything is o.k. now and that the roads are open and passable. We are dining early tonight at a famous Chinese restaurant which is called by a Japanese name now for obvious reasons. Then back to pack and to bed early so we will be ready for anything tomorrow.

≋ six

June 25, Sikkim

FROM Calcutta we took a smaller plane for the hour's flight to Bagdogra, where we were met by two tiny Sikkimese men. The Indians we saw in Delhi were about the same size as most Americans, and some Indians are very tall and big; these men seemed minute by comparison. They have the wide flattish faces of the Mongols, Tibetans and our Eskimos, and the coloring of the American Indian, brown skin and red cheeks. But though short, they are sturdy and strong; tough, wiry mountain people.

Our new escorts took us quickly through the airport red tape, we climbed into a jeep, Harrison and I in front with the driver, and off we went for a six hour drive, up and down, back and forth, half in daylight, half in the dark, across a mountain, down into the valley, up again, over and over until we finally reached Gangtok at about eight. The regular route takes only three hours but the roads had been badly damaged in the recent heavy rains so we had to take this longer detour. At the border between India and Sikkim we stopped at the Sikkim Distillery and had a cup of tea with the manager and his wife. He suggested the local wine and when we got here we were told we had been wise to choose tea; the liquor is terrible—they sell it to India.

Before it got dark we drove up and down mountains planted with rice in tiny paddies that looked like pictures of Japan, every inch used; what isn't in rice has some other crop. I have never seen terraced farming on such steep slopes, all so neat and precise, and more of that beautiful bright green. Harrison said there must be other places where farming would be easier, but Hope told us today that Gangtok was chosen for the capital because it is relatively flat for Sikkim and the flattest place is about as big as a soccer field.

We arrived at eight after winding up what seemed a topless mountain, through the lights and the city, up through a gate with brightly-dressed guards, up some more to the palace. The mist was so thick we could scarcely see and I was conscious only of a porch that reminded me of my grandmother's house with potted geraniums on the steps. A palace functionary came running, greeted us, took us indoors, and ran down a corridor. A tiny whisper floated from upstairs, "Mrs. Salisbury, Mrs. Salisbury. . . ." We looked up and there was our hostess, the Gyalmo, Hope Cooke, in her wrapper, leaning over the railing. "I'm sorry I'm not dressed," she said. At that her husband the Chogyal, appeared, bowing and apologizing, and showed us upstairs and said, "My wife will be ready soon." He is very attractive. We had coffee and a drink, unpacked, and Hope came in to say hello. Everyone had said she talks in a low voice but we weren't prepared for how low it actually is. Amazing thing—with my bad ear I can hear her better than Harrison can.

We talked a bit, then bathed and changed as there was a big dinner party with all the government people to celebrate Hope's twenty-sixth birthday. Thank goodness I had a long skirt made in Delhi. We all sat around the room on low sofas and ate off beautiful little carved and painted tables, after serving ourselves from a buffet table. The guests included the Indian Army General in command of this district, tall and handsome in his uniform (he had passed us at the border in an army jeep that had gone right through blowing a siren; if we had known, we could have flown direct from Delhi with him and avoided Calcutta), the man in charge of the roads, also in uniform (he is very busy now due to all the storm damage), and the Prime Minister who, too, is Indian, and other council members and their wives. The Indian women wore saris and the Sikkimese women wore their traditional dress, a long sleeveless dress pulled to the back in an inverted fold and held by a belt over a long-sleeved blouse. The older women wear their hair in braids. The Sikkimese men wear a long coat that fastens with frogs at the neck and on the side, also with a belt. They wear this over trousers. After dinner we sat on the porch in the mist and listened to a band playing the Sikkim instruments which sound like bagpipes.

This morning at eight we had our "bed tea" and quite a lot later, breakfast, boiled eggs, toast and coffee. The servants wear all different sorts of outfits and sometimes a soldier brings things. H. said, "A paratrooper has brought breakfast."

We are in the palace guest room, a big square room, like a guest room in any house I have stayed in at home, except it has only a skylight, no windows. The house, which is a rambling, wood, country house, was designed by an architect who thought the bathrooms should be on the outside with outside staircases leading to them so it would be easy for the servants to get in for cleaning. The furniture in our room is all New England; maple beds and a Winthrop type desk. The only exotic touch is a low sort of bed couch with bright pillows and a cover of long white fur. Our bathroom has windows on two sides and a door opening out, as well as the door going in from our room. Besides the usual bathroom fixtures, it has a urinal which makes a great gurgling noise and is called Old Faithful, and a washing machine which is being used at the moment as a store house for toilet articles impossible to buy in this mountain kingdom.

June 26, West Sikkim

How do I describe today? Is it today, or yesterday, or one hundred years ago? Is it the *King and I* in Sikkim, is it a dream? How can it be today and be real? But it is both, because we are standing right in the middle of the unreality along with the Gyalmo who is also Hope Cooke, friend of Ellen at Sarah Lawrence College; riding in jeeps; drinking Scotch and House of Lords gin; reading a copy of the *Hindustan Times;* talking about India, China, Russia,

75

Vietnam; talking to the queen and an Indian lady about Dr. Spock and bringing up children. My first impression of Asia was of conglomeration, mixture, something of everything either stirred up together or in pieces or layers, and Sikkim is no exception.

We spent the day driving over and around, up and down, one mountain after another, leaving some time after nine o'clock, heading for a rendezvous with the Chogyal who had been away in India since yesterday. Before jeeps, travel was with mules, ponies, or on foot, and every few miles there was a stop and resting place for travellers. If the travellers were the royal family, there was a special welcome and celebration and many refreshments—tea, beer, cakes and anything special the area had to offer. Where before it took two or three hours to cover a certain distance, now it takes about twenty minutes to half an hour. Yesterday all along our route the people had planned receptions and we made five or six stops before lunch and several afterwards. Usually some distance before the village, children stood at intervals on either side of the road, tending fires of juniper or some spicy plant. At the entrance a gate would be decorated with greens and flowers and a sign "Welcome" on top. The village bands were out to announce our arrival. These consist of large, beautiful, curved horns and the reed-like instruments that sound like bagpipes, drums and cymbals. The cars stopped, everyone got out and scarves were presented to the Gyalmo by the village elders. Bowing, each offers her a long, white scarf with both hands; Her Highness takes it with both hers, bows in return and gives it back. Only on special occasions does she keep the scarf. The children gave her bouquets and ropes of flowers and then we walked to a table laden with refreshments. Harrison and

I went along and were treated as honored guests, too. We had tea at each stop and Her Highness always had a sip of the beer (chang). This is made by pouring warm water onto fermented millet. It is made and served in a tall bamboo container and sipped through a bamboo reed. The two year old Prince Palden, who, with his Tibetan nurse, accompanied us (his mother thinking the bumpy jeep ride might cure him of his love for cars), also took part at every stop, drank tea, ate crackers and roasted corn, always wanted more and never got tired. At most of the stops a carpet of material, anchored with stones, was laid down for us to walk on—gaily printed cottons in all colors; at some places, velvet and silk. We walked on such a carpet through a whole village to the house of a wiry, determined-looking woman, a rich widow who seemed very influential, up some steps and into her sitting room. The walls and ceiling were also covered with fabric and a large picture of President Kennedy was prominently displayed.

We met the Chogyal at a clearing by a rushing mountain river, down a steep path from the road. He sat under a tree, dressed in a white bakku (the Sikkim dress), patiently waiting; he had been there three hours already. A typical Asian picnic was cooked and served by the mountain rangers—rice, chicken and beans, other mysterious concoctions, mangos and bananas.

After lunch we proceeded on our drive, stopping every so often, and at each stop the Chogyal made a short speech to the crowds. We reached our destination, the Pamoinchi DAK cottage on top of a mountain, at six o'clock. This is one of many bungalows built by the British in northern India and the Himalayan countries to accommodate travellers to those remote regions where there were no inns or

77

hostels. They were run by the government and guests had to have permission to stay, also were required to bring all their bedding and food. They are similar in design; a covered porch leads into a central room where there is a long table for dining, and three bedrooms open off this room. There is no running water but hot and cold are brought whenever we want; we have a tin tub for bathing, a washstand and pitchers and a thunderbox john. An enormous towel rack is in one corner of our bathroom with one bath towel, hand towel and wash cloth for H. and me. There is no electricity; candles and oil lanterns are the lights. The Prime Minister of Sikkim and his sister, a charming Indian lady who went to Columbia, dined with us. We are all tired after the long day of driving and visiting and H. and I have just taken baths in the tin tub and are going to sleep.

June 28

FOR the last two days we have accompanied their Highnesses on a very strenuous tour of villages, schools, a hospital, farm projects and monasteries. Harrison says it is like campaigning with Kennedy and the Chogyal does make me think of him; a young, attractive intelligent man, popular with his people and concerned about his country.

In the morning, at about eight, the fire in our fireplace is lit and tea is brought to us in bed (it is lovely to wake up to these luxuries) and later we have breakfast with our host and hostess, then off on the day's visits. On our trip on Sunday with the Gyalmo, we had six jeeps in our party. Since combining forces with the Chogyal there are fifteen jeeps and a jeep station wagon. A yellow pilot jeep with red flags on the hood precedes us and the others follow, everywhere we go, and all the passengers get out at every stop and join in the ceremonies. I can't make out who all the people are but the group includes members of the government, the chief medical officer, a successful contractor who is a de-frocked monk and whose nickname is Al Capone, a young man we met on the way up from Bagdogra, and a large contingent of the Sikkim army.

Yesterday we first attended a service in the Monastery which is just above here. The Chogyal and the Gyalmo sat on the side behind high tables strewn with flowers and laden with delicacies; we sat at a table lower down; the rest of the entourage sat around the sides and the monks were in two rows down the middle facing the Buddha. Tea was served to everyone except the monks, who chanted in the most re-sounding bass voices—a rapid, consistent sort of chattering chant. At times they sounded like several auctioneers in uni-son. These were tea prayers. When they were finished we drank the tea and inspected the murals which, though newly painted, are the same old forms and designs and colors that paintings and decorations depicting the life and travail of the Buddha have always been.

Next we visited a government agricultural project and saw samples of rice, wheat, corn, vegetables and fruits, farming implements, fertilizers, etc. Corn grows wonder-fully here, very tall and straight, marching up the terraced mountain sides like tin soldiers. Again, as in Cambodia, I am surprised it grows so well where it is so wet. I think it is amazing what the Sikkimese do with such limited space, but the Chogyal seemed critical of a lot of the program; he seemed to feel they hadn't accomplished as much as they should have at this time. As usual we sat down to tea and refreshments. Cucumbers grow to over a foot here and look like a large green squash but, strangely, the slices were crisp and delicious, not at all woody and soft the way I would expect.

After that we inspected a hospital, a good solid building sensibly planned. Every room has wide windows and is big and airy. Being used to our hospitals, I was surprised to see a red wool blanket on the operating table, but then I thought of how many infections (staph, for instance) people pick up in our white, shiny and supposedly antiseptic hospitals. With no running water it is a great achievement to have a hospital as clean and neat as this one we saw. Most of the patients were sitting up in bed wearing their own colored clothes and, with two or three exceptions, didn't look very sick. I believe they care mostly for emergencies and the prevalent intestinal disorders here; operations and more serious illnesses are done and cared for in Gangtok.

From there we drove until the road was impassable even for jeeps, got out and walked through the jungle to the site of an old palace, built in the seventeenth century, which belonged to the Chogyal's family. It was destroyed during the fighting with the British in the early 1900's. The walk in was lovely, if steep, and we saw several beautiful small orchids we have never seen before (Sikkim has more than six hundred known types of orchids). As we walked we saw remains of the old walls and suddenly the jungle opened up to what had been the site of the actual palace. I felt we were on top of the world until I looked up and there was the monastery we'd been to in the morning, above us. It gave a protective feeling; the old palace, even on top of this particular peak, was still under the wing, so to speak, of the monastery.

There were tents and all the equipment which we now expect with picnics. A lunch of sandwiches, fruit and a cold drink will seem pretty measly after the picnics we have had in Asia.

After lunch we visited a school, a well laid out building on a beautiful site. From the large windows there are such breath-taking views of the mountains I would find it hard to keep my eyes on anything inside the room. We stopped in several classes and the Chogyal demonstrated again his interest and skill in meeting and talking with his people. He asked questions, looked at some of the children's papers and led lively discussions on the subjects they were studying. He does all this, countryside politiking I suppose we would call it, so well; his heart is really in it.

At seven we returned to the school for their entertainment. It was like any school show anywhere; it might have been one of the many I have been to in the course of bringing up four children. We sat in the front row of the balcony; downstairs were the children not taking part in the performance, parents, friends, teachers. Except for some of the clothes, it might have been an audience watching a school entertainment in a small town in Kansas. Most of the girls wear ordinary dresses or blouses and skirts, and the boys wear shirts and either long or short pants. The adults are usually in bakkus or in the bright wraps and folds of the Nepal skirts, but here and there you see a western type dress. The program was a variety of short scenes, recitations and dances. Several were in English and one about boy scouts was very funny. The accents are atrocious and very hard to understand. This seems to be a problem; they can't get teachers with good accents; India won't allow people to come in. Here is where a U. S. Peace Corps program could contribute enormously, yet it isn't permitted. I can't understand this; help with their schools, as well as with the agricultural projects, would be invaluable. It is too bad.

From the site of the old palace where we had lunch yesterday we saw a symmetrical steep mountain rising up like a pyramid amidst the more irregular jagged forms. This is Rangacholing mountain and the site of the new monastery which is to be built to replace the original which burned four years ago. We started early this morning to attend the ceremonies for laying the cornerstone and drove for a while, then walked through the jungly woods to a partial clearing. No matter how brief the stop or how hidden and remote the place, there is always the presenting of scarves and gifts and flowers to their Highnesses, and here a group was waiting for us. From there to the top seemed straight up, like a ladder, and there were horses for the Chogyal and the Gyalmo, Harrison and me and a few of the less rugged, to ride. The others dashed up the rocky cliff like mountain goats and arrived before we did. I didn't see how I could get on a horse, let alone sit astride, in my skirt which is short, tight and unsuitable for this part of the world, and I couldn't wear slacks as it is not appropriate for women. So I brought along a pair of H's pants, slipped them on over everything for the riding and felt comfortable and relieved. Hope wore a pink brocade bakku and light blue silk blouse for her day of walking, climbing, riding and helping with all the ceremonies and, amazingly, looked lovely and unmussed at the end of it all.

At the top, monks in their red-brown robes greeted us

and we marched to the accompaniment of horns and drums in a procession to a small chapel for a service with chanting similar to yesterday's. Prayer flags fluttered among the gray stupas surrounding the trenches, freshly dug for the foundation of the new monastery. A stone was laid at each corner, one between these on each side, and one in the center—nine stones in all. Under each was put a brightly-colored, decorated urn, grain, rice, pine and scarves. When everything was laid in properly, more rice was sprinkled on top and the Chogyal cemented it over, applying the cement with a gorgeous silver trowel. It was hot, hard work and took over two hours. It is difficult to describe these ceremonies as so much is happening all the time and I don't know what most of it means. There couldn't be many places left in the world where there are such colorful ceremonies and we feel privileged and lucky to have been here to see and take part in one. And take part we did, after lunch, when everyone was full of food, liquor and good will. We joined in a big dance, a threshing dance. The step is simply stamping one's feet more or less in rhythm and usually it is rather boring to do and to watch. But lots of feeling had been generated by the local liquor and it was as lively as some of our country dances at home.

For lunch we each had a big platter with five bowls of different foods and a huge pile of rice, all covered up with a large leaf called a commercial leaf. When we were finished we covered the platter again with the leaf and no one could tell how little we had eaten. We have had so many curries and so many strange, hot and greasy dishes, sometimes I long for a plain broiled chicken and a green salad which is safe to eat.

On the way back to the DAK we visited a boarding

school for boys. It was the same kind of nice, open, airy building as the hospital and school we have seen and looked just about like any camp or dormitory—the same beds and blankets, books, pictures and junk that all boys all over the world have to have. At night we had a dinner for the monks and the people in the area who have entertained us. The party mood still prevailed; there was dancing and singing and the guests stayed until one o'clock.

I keep feeling as if I were at a Sarah Lawrence play watching Ellen and her friends in their latest production. I know this setting is real and certainly the characters are real, but still there is such an atmosphere of unreality. I keep thinking this play will be over soon, the curtains will close on the stage, I will say goodnight and take the 11:54 train back to New York.

In this strange mixture of real and unreal Hope fits in as if she had always been a part of it. In a setting where most Americans would stand out conspicuously, she blends right into the background, moving in a slightly bowing, sideways walk, looking strangely Eastern and Western at the same time. She always appears in the Sikkimese dress, and, nodding and smiling and making little clucking noises, makes everyone feel she understands even when she doesn't. She is well informed about her new country and works hard to interpret its problems and needs to the West. The people seem very proud of her, as we are too. It is a demanding role. Along with the fairy tale romance of her life with the Chogyal in this tiny mountain kingdom, she is isolated and must be very lonely at times.

June 29, 9 a.m.

FOR once I am all ready, packed and waiting, and their Highnesses are still asleep. The household is also ready and anxious to leave; all are worried about the roads as it is raining and may be very slippery. Evidently it was clear at seven and the high Himalayas were visible, but no one woke us up. Too bad, but maybe we will come here again someday.

June 30, Gangtok

WE TOOK off from the Pamoinchi DAK at about 10:30 yesterday morning in rain coming down in sheets. First the yellow pilot jeep with red flags and soldiers; next the Chogyal driving, Hope and I in front and the baby and his nurse in back; a jeep of soldiers next, then Harrison and the Chogyal's young and beautiful brother-in-law, and so on for fifteen jeeps. Several of the monks and a few local people had come to say goodby. Most of the servants travelled with us, along with the royal retinue, members of the government, the chief medical officer and others. As usual, a small band played and those wonderful horns that only sound right in the mountains followed us as we drove down the hairpin curves of the road. At intervals people stood by the side waving and cheering, and soon the rain stopped and the clouds lifted though the sun never came out. Although the weather was terrible, we were late in starting and had a long way to go, we stopped at every place the Chogyal was expected; he didn't pass by any. At several villages he was presented with baskets of ferns and mushrooms, bamboo shoots and other delicacies; also a little barking deer in a crate. The custom is that if the Chogyal accepts what is offered him, which he always seems to, he has to give the people in return a gift of equal value plus twenty percent.

Again we stopped at the village of the strong-willed lady where Hope and Harrison and I had been before. That day there had been velvet and silk for us to walk on but today the carpet that wound through the village was of burlap with cotton on top—more suitable for the wet weather. First we had tea and refreshments at the entrance of the town. Then we walked through it and up to the lady's house and again sat with pictures of Nehru and Kennedy looking down on us. More refreshments here and the biggest pig I ever saw was dragged in (dead and cleaned and ready for cutting up and cooking). It must have weighed at least two hundred pounds and, with all the other gifts, was loaded on top of the luggage.

When we were full of tea and snacks, for even if you just nibble and sip you consume a certain amount, we got into the jeep again and drove about one hundred yards to another DAK where we had lunch. The meal was the usual; many dishes of strange concoctions and two kinds of rice.

After lunch we stopped at the tea plantation. This was started a few years ago to provide occupation for Tibetan refugees from the Chinese, and because Sikkim wants a tea industry. In the past the British preferred to grow tea only in Assam and Darjeeling. Many acres have already been cleared and planted with tea and they hope to have one thousand acres under cultivation eventually. Very nice houses have been built for the refugees with the kitchens under a separate roof just behind each main house. We had refreshments twice here, first with the manager, and right afterwards down the hill under a shelter. Baskets of delicacies were presented here also, and although it was raining hard again everyone stood around outside, oblivious of the weather. They must be accustomed to it—being wet probably feels as natural as being dry. The young prince Palden handed out candy to all the children and two sets of dances were performed for us. By this time we were all pretty disheveled and in varying states of dampness.

Next stop was a school we hadn't had time to stop at on the way over. We walked behind the local band and VIPs through the street, then suddenly took off down an eighty degree angle cliff and more or less slid down to the school house. The path was covered with boughs of pine and leaves and that helped some, but my feet would catch in the branches and if it hadn't been for a strong man who gripped my arm in an iron grasp, holding it up so high I was tipping over sideways, I would have fallen many times. Here again, we had an entertainment, but it was cut short as it was getting late, raining off and on, and we still had a long way to go. Getting back up the slippery slope was solved for Hope and me by having a cloth put around our waists, each end held tightly by a sturdy mountain lad, and thus we were conveyed up to the top. The Chogyal said, "Lean back and make use of it," and after the initial strangeness, it felt extremely comfortable and was almost like being wafted on air; I only had to move my feet to keep up with the rest of me.

Before climbing back into the jeep I noticed some black splotches on my legs and thinking they were dirt, reached down to brush them off. They not only didn't brush off, they felt wet and slimy. Leeches—a real pest in Sikkim —were firmly attached to my skin and sucking my blood. Everyone rushed to help and they were pulled off and thrown away. It would be hard to squash them and Buddhists would probably not do that anyway. Salt was produced to rub on the spots and I had no ill effects except the feeling of revulsion.

It was now starting to get dark and raining hard and there were thirty-five more miles to go; back and forth, up and down, never a straight stretch more than two hundred yards, if that. It is incredible how the Sikkimese drive so skillfully but, as they say, either you drive well or you go over the cliffs; there is no choice. With the Chogyal driving I was never nervous. Even looking straight down thousands of feet from the narrow, rocky, zig zag mountain roads I felt as safe as if I were driving with Harrison around the peaceful Connecticut countryside. His Highness is a remarkable man—so capable and versatile—a jack of all trades and master of them all, from driving to fixing the palace plumbing, cooking an omelette for us and managing the household. He is no millionaire monarch with castles and airplanes and polo ponies living high off the sweat of his people; he is a kind, simple man of his time with a twentieth century point of view, doing his best to improve the lives of the people he governs.

We made several more brief stops and always the villagers were lined up with scarves and flowers, the bands playing and the children singing, no matter how hard the rain came down. They hold their hands together as if praying and shut their eyes when they sing. I noticed two little girls with red nail polish. Many of the women have jewelry in their noses and ears and wear the Nepal type of dress. All along the road people stood in order to catch a glimpse of their Highnesses. Often they had umbrellas, usually black, but occasionally the large multi-colored umbrellas I associate with Abercrombie and Fitch, and fancy golf clubs.

Although the DAK in West Sikkim is only seventy-five miles from Gangtok, it took nearly eleven hours for our trip. But considering the many stops we made, the weather and the condition of the roads, I wonder it didn't take longer. In spite of the torrential rain only one place in the road had washed away but it had been patched up, Heaven knows how, with oil drums and stones, so it was just possible to get over. Here, for the first time, I didn't dare look, although I probably couldn't have seen anything but rushing water. It was raining, foggy and dark.

At this break in the road we realized many people had gathered, to help or to watch, or just to be there. It seemed far from a village or settlement, but by the flickering lanterns and flashlights we could see them, under umbrellas, in the branch of a tree above the road, along the side which hadn't yet washed away, or standing in the rushing water. There are always people all over the place, here and everywhere we've been in Southeast Asia. Even in the woods and jungles people pop out of nowhere and one wonders where they have been. This, of course, is one of the hazards in Vietnam. The Vietnamese belong there and can blend with or vanish into the landscape while we are out of place and awkward and have to burn people out of their hiding places or defoliate large areas so we can see. Everything in Asia is done with and by everybody, all milling around and jabbering in shrill voices as in Hong Kong, or moving quietly, talking in whispers, or just standing, as here in Sikkim.

Back at last, at the palace, after hot baths and drinks and a very late supper, we all felt better, but I don't think I will ever feel completely dry again.

Today we have had a pleasant day doing nothing much. Harrison saw a few people and talked to the Chogyal in his office; we visited the Tibetan Institute where they are carrying on Buddhist studies which no longer are allowed in Tibet; Hope took me to two schools, and we bought a few things at their cottage industries. The Gyalmo has helped to create what should turn into a substantial business for her country. Rugs, tables, all sorts of woodwork, dolls and toys, are among the articles made by the Sikkim men and women, and unusual paper and natural native materials. The dyes are made from plants and roots and the colors are earthy and natural; some strong and robust, others pale and delicate. The schools seem up to date and well-equipped and both had good libraries with many books in English. Guests came for supper and "home" movies, which included films taken by the Chogyal in Tibet in 1954 and 1956 before the Chinese closed their borders.

We have eaten all our lunches and dinners here at the palace in the small living room, sitting on low sofas or chairs, with a carved, painted Sikkimese table in front of each person. When there have been just the four of us, servants have brought in trays and passed the dishes; when there were other guests we helped ourselves from a buffet and returned, each to his place. It is informal and cozy and makes everyone feel at ease. Their Highnesses hardly ever sit at the long table in the dining room.

Tonight for the movies we dined in the big living room,

sitting on the brocade-covered sofas and chairs, eating from trays. At one end of the room the Chogyal helped put up the projector and showed the films himself, carefully explaining each picture to us. His first wife, who died, was Tibetan and they had made trips to Tibet, first by horse caravan, then with jeeps. There were pictures of enormous sweeps of pale beige plains surrounded by mountains; beautiful flowers and animals and birds and a procession of monks and a ceremony of macabre dances in costumes—probably never before photographed.

This afternoon at one of the schools we visited, a girls' school for grades one through six, I saw a big blackboard on the covered porch just outside the front door with these news items printed in large white letters:

1) U.S. BOMBS HANOI AND HAIPHONG
2) CHINA WARNS SHE WILL ENTER WAR IF BOMBING PERSISTS
3) INDIA CONCERNED OVER U.S. BOMBING

This is how I learned of this recent attack. When I got back to the palace I found Harrison, who had heard it reported over the wireless. We feel as if we had been hit, and hit again, hard. We are stunned, ashamed. I had begun to feel (I suppose because we are out of touch with home and I have been allowing myself to drift into a state of unrealistic thinking as far as the United States is concerned) that by some miracle the people in Washington would realize that dropping bombs does the opposite of what they want; it strengthens the will to resist and it does irreparable damage to our image and reputation all over the world, especially in Asia. What will happen next? I am sick with disgust and horror.

July 1, Noon

WE STARTED off this morning at eight to return to Delhi but about a half-hour from here we were stopped by a landslide and had to come back. There have been terrible rains and the wires and telephones are all down; there is no way of communicating with anyone; we are stranded. They are trying to get a wire out for H. and we are hoping (pretty much in vain I think) to get some distance by to-night so we can fly back tomorrow. But it is noon already and there is no sign of any change or improvement.

July 2, On the plane from Calcutta to Delhi

YESTERDAY we waited all day for some break or change, but in vain, as I had feared. Finally at six o'clock, the man in charge of the roads and an engineer who looks like Nelson Rockefeller, came to discuss the situation. On the basis of the most recent reports it was decided we would start at four a.m. and take a long circuitous route which would mean twelve or more hours of driving—a depressing prospect but better than doing any night driving. We were having dinner and watching more movies when the handsome General in charge of this area, who had been at dinner our first night here, telephoned and said the roads would be passable tomorrow; if there were places impossible to drive over, we could walk, he would have jeeps and drivers on the other side, and if we started at seven a.m. he would personally guarantee that we would get to Bagdogra by one thirty to catch the plane to Calcutta. Two jeeps would come for us in the morning.

That was very comforting and we went back to watching the movies. This evening we saw pictures of the coronation here in 1964, made by BBC and narrated by Roderick MacFarquar. It is too bad it isn't in color. The pictures taken inside the temple were lovely and would have been so beautiful.

Certainly the Chogyal and Hope have been extraordinarily hospitable and kind to us. They are wonderful hosts. I don't think there are many things more trying than guests who stay longer than expected, no matter what the reason, and they have never let us feel anything but the same warmth and concern for our comfort that we have felt all during this visit.

This morning we left again, in a jeep with our luggage and a big, strong, green-turbanned driver, preceded by an Army captain and two soldiers in a pilot jeep. It was overcast and cloudy and raining off and on and there were terrible washouts and landslides which were just barely passable. We came to one where we had to wait while the road crew cleared one place and filled in another, which took about half an hour. The road repair gangs are unique; they seem to be made up of anyone who happens along and are usually young boys, women in their pretty long clothes, little girls and several men. The women are often sitting by a big stone, hammering it into fragments for fill, which are then put on the sides of the road in neat, uniform size pieces for use when necessary. Large picks and hoes are the most common implements. When it rains hard all work stops and everyone stands under umbrellas until the rain lets up. Just after we got to this place it started to pour so the job was delayed for a while. It was too wet to get out and stretch so we just waited in the jeep.

After about two and a half hours we came to an army camp where the road forked. We were told the regular road was impassable; we were to take another route and would have to walk across a road block. Another jeep would be waiting for us on the other side. We drove a bit and as we approached the block a handsome captain stopped us and said he was to relieve our present army escorts and would accompany us from there, across the block and to the airport. He had our names on a piece of paper, more to be sure about our name than, I imagine, to be sure we were the right travellers; there were no others.

Around the corner and half way up a hill we saw the road block. We drove up to it and my heart sank; the road was solid rocks, trees, and earth—a terrible landslide—and not even a mountain goat could have crossed it with any assurance of making it alive. Matter-of-factly our new captain said, "We will blast that, then walk across." So the jeeps were backed up about one hundred yards; we all walked back a little further, stepped off the road and stood behind a tree about fifteen inches in diameter. It didn't look like much protection but nobody seemed to question the safety of this whole enterprise and it turned out they were right. On top of the road block quite a few people were scrambling about and a tall Indian man, dressed in white and a bright turban, began to blow a whistle. This was the blasting warning, and when all had dispersed we heard and saw the first explosion. Rocks, stones, trees, everything, flew into the air, whirled around a bit, then settled down in just the same places as before. A second blast with what looked like the same result, and I waited for the third to go off. Evidently there was to be no third explosion for the Captain said, "All right, we'll go now," so we went along behind him to the still trembling and smoking road block. Obviously we couldn't go near the edge—there wasn't even six inches flat to put your foot on and the cliff went straight down for what looked like a mile at least. He stepped along as if he were walking on a side walk—straight up the steaming mass, saying, "This way." Once more the short, tight American skirt was against me. Never again will I travel to Asia without some fairly long and moderately full skirts; they protect one from so much that is obvious—and from the unexpected postures one finds oneself in—sitting on the floor, climbing up on a horse, scrambling up and down road blocks. Not being so equipped, I just forgot about it and on all fours crawled up behind the captain and down the other side. Somehow or other Harrison made it on his two feet, even taking pictures, but he wrenched his knee. Our bags were carried *across*, as they said; it looked straight up and straight down to me. On the other side was a flock of sheep and goats, waiting until it was safer to cross.

This time we had one jeep. The Captain sat in back and we were in front with the driver who seemed nervous. I didn't blame him, but it made me nervous, too. Slipping around in muddy ruts on the edge of a precipice with a driver who lacks confidence is unsettling. However, all went well. The road follows the river, which surged wildly; it went many times faster than we did, with violent rapids and swells that looked like a stormy ocean except it was a light brown, like coffee with milk, from all the earth that had washed down the mountain sides.

Everything was under control; there were no more road blocks, we got down on the flat, miraculously, with just enough time to get to the airport, and we ran out of gas. Indians believe in astrology and the stars, and certainly Harrison's and mine, though we have different signs, must all have been in the right place at that moment because a Red Cross jeep came by, was flagged, stopped, our captain jumped in and disappeared. We walked up and down the road, each trying to pretend we weren't worried and struggling to be cheerful, until our captain returned in still another jeep, with two tanks of gas and another very attractive young captain. The tank was filled but the jeep wouldn't start, so all our stuff was moved to the latest jeep, and, with the new captain driving, we set off at a terrific clip. Just as we started there were several loud backfires from the other jeep and it came bounding after us. It was now ten to one—the plane was due in five minutes and scheduled to leave at one twenty and we had twenty minutes more driving to do, plus all the things you have to take care of at an airport—luggage, tickets, and explain why we wanted seats today though our tickets were for yesterday. It was a wild ride and thank heaven for our newest captain-driver. He was a wonder. All this time, though we all had thought about it, no one mentioned the possibility that the plane might not be flying. It was bad enough to think about privately, but it would have been too much to discuss. Yet after all, there had been storms, floods, dense fog, everything that makes bad flying conditions.

We were racing along, feeling encouraged, when we got to a railroad crossing with the gates down and no sign of a train from any direction. On the way up we had been

Harrison on a street corner in Hong Kong,
but feeling as if he were at the Chinese border

Water wheel irrigation, typical of Cambodia

Phnom Penh: on the steps of Wat Phnom

Angkor: heavenly dancing girls—Aspara

Demons at the gate of Angkor Thom

Bangkok: Thai child on
the steps of her house
at the edge of the klong

Bangkok: coal barges on the klong

Rangoon: mother and son at the Shwe Dagon Pagoda

Rangoon: the Shwe Dagon Pagoda

Rangoon: children playing in the Pagoda

Mandalay: pupil performing at the dancing school

The author at the Taj Mahal

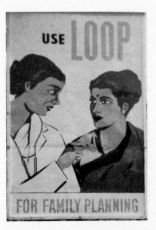

New Delhi: poster on billboard

The Royal Family on tour in west Sikkim

Sikkim: the Chogyal and the Gyalmo
at the dedication of Rangacholing Monastery

Dance after the dedication ceremonies,
Rangacholing Monastery

Mongolia: survivors of the flood reassembling their homes

Ulan Bator:
Mongolian man
and his horse

Temple in Ulan Bator

stopped for about half an hour on the other side. There had been no sign of any train then, either, and we had walked up and down and wondered about Asians and their ways of doing things, so different from ours, and were amused. This time we were not amused; we still had about two miles to go and it was well after one o'clock. I felt so dirty and grubby; our bags were covered with mud; inside our clothes were still wet from being caught in the rain so often and not getting dried and they must have been mildewing fast as we had packed Thursday night and here it was Saturday noon. The thought of another night, probably spent at the airport, filled me with despair. And Harrison really needed to get back to Delhi, which was much more important than my feelings and the condition of our belongings.

The captain turned off the engine and sat back as if this were a routine trip to the village to get the morning mail. Our other captain behind got out and wandered casually across the tracks to one of those sort of sentry box houses and vanished. Still no sign of a train—no sign of anything except the shut gates and the captain's wrist watch. All the time it was raining. A little boy came out of the sentry box house, put up a huge umbrella and walked up the track. After a few more minutes which seemed more like hours, the captain who had vanished returned with good news. He had called the airport, the plane wasn't in yet, it was on its way. They expected us and would wait for us and we would have time to eat lunch in the airport restaurant.

With that the gates went up, the collection of people, bicycles, jeeps, trucks, crossed the tracks, and we drove the remaining distance to the airport. Everything went as he had said; the plane came in, we had lunch at a table next to the pilot and the stewardesses, we said goodbye and thanks to our army friends and flew off to Calcutta. We wondered, as we settled back in the plane, if a train ever did pass that railroad crossing.

 *seven*

July 7, New Delhi

WE HAVE been back here for a few days gathering together ourselves, our belongings and our thoughts, and trying to work through all the obstacles and red tape and get on with this trip. We can't seem to get visas for Russia, either regular or transit, and if we can't, then we won't be able to continue on our swing around China, which is a big blow. We had hoped to go to Moscow, Mongolia and Siberia, take the Trans-Siberian Railroad and then continue on by boat to Japan. Oh dear, it sounds so romantic and exciting and would be such fun. We have been delayed by changing plans and the weather, and are way behind on our schedule. We had counted on the Indian travel agent here to have everything fixed up for us by the time we came back from Sikkim but it didn't work out that way. He is so good-looking and nice, comes up to see us, smiles, says he is in touch with Moscow and we aren't to worry, but nothing seems to happen. Our reservations are for tomorrow and we are all packed and ready to leave, hoping our friend is right.

July 8, Airport at New Delhi, 10:15 a.m.

WE ARE waiting for the plane to Moscow, which is already an hour late. We still have no visas but the travel agent and the people at the Russian Embassy said that transit visas would be at the Moscow airport for us when we arrived. We can stay in Moscow two days and get our Mongolian visas renewed, as they expired yesterday and we couldn't do anything about it here. If all this fails, Harrison says we can go to London, then home. Certainly there are worse fates, but it isn't what he wants at this point.

July 10, Ulan Bator, Mongolia

WE ARE in a de luxe suite in the Ulan Bator Hotel in Ulan Bator, the capital of Mongolia. If, on Friday morning in New Delhi, anyone had said this is where we would be in thirty-six hours I would have said he was crazy. And the whole experience has been crazy, ridiculous.

We had a pleasant, comfortable flight from Delhi to Moscow; we went first class for some unexplained reason, for our tickets are economy all the way. This trip has shown me the pointlessness in asking anything, except in extreme situations, but even then it doesn't do any good, doesn't change anything and doesn't explain anything. I like to know where I am, what I am supposed to do, why, and what is coming next, and all the time I have to fight down the desire to try and find out. We are always getting into cars, driving off to unknown places with people we can't communicate with, trusting everything to strangers, and somehow or other it all works out one way or another—not always the way we had planned or expected or hoped, but usually all right, and a proof each time of the waste of energy to question anything or to worry.

It was very clear so we got a wonderful look at northern India, Pakistan, Afghanistan—huge snow-covered mountains, red, dusty plains, the pale, sandy desert and then the deep and beautiful green of Russia. It is so vast, so enormous and endless. I keep hearing that by the year two thousand there will be standing room only on this planet, but even if the population explosion continues at the present rate, I can't imagine that these areas will be filled up. There were only occasional dots of human life in hours of flying. It was refreshing to see the tall straight pines and firs of Russia after all the climbing, twisting jungle growth we have been in, and to imagine the cool, clear air. But imagining was all I could do. We never got out of the Moscow airport except to get aboard another plane.

The *New York Times* correspondent, Peter Grose, and Sara, the Russian girl Harrison had hired in 1954 as translator and secretary for the *Times*, met us, and for six hours, while I sat in the waiting room, they and H. struggled with the rules and regulations and red tape of the rigid Communist system. Perhaps we are as bad; it is hard to believe. Our transit visas were not there, no one had heard of us, it was too late on Saturday afternoon to get any official help, we were definitely not wanted and would have to leave on the next plane for Mongolia. They would give us visas, but only the kind for getting out of Russia. Policemen, Intourist people, telephone operators and airport officials, one or two polite, many rude, the rest just doing their cut and dried job with no feeling, were involved in getting us out. The police took our passports, the airport officials our tickets; someone else had the exit visas, and so on. Miraculously, just in time, all our papers came back at once and we got on the plane for Irkutsk, Siberia. It was 9:30 Moscow time and I guess about midnight New Delhi time. I am still very confused but as we were in or near the land of the midnight sun it wasn't dark for very long no matter what time it was. We were given a plain but good meal starting off with a huge glob of fresh caviar and we slept off and on in the bright light.

All planes in Russia are met by a doctor in case anyone is ill. Our two flights were met by attractive, capable-looking, young women doctors. At Irkutsk, after the doctor made sure no one was sick, a woman guide led all the passengers to the airport building, up some stairs and into a dining-room. There another efficient woman took charge and showed us where to sit. No empty places were allowed; a table had to be filled before people started to sit at another. Fortunately Harrison and I got at the same table. After our breakfast of three hardboiled eggs each, bread, butter, tea and kefir, which is a kind of sour, clotted milk, we were led by our first guide to two adjoining waiting rooms and we waited in one of them for three hours for the plane to Ulan Bator. I felt as if I were back in grade school with competent teachers and nurses waiting to guide me at every turn.

While we were waiting, Harrison heard an American voice and, investigating, found it to be Bernie Reisman of ABC. He had had permission, papers, visas, everything in order for Mongolia, and had gone in with men and equipment to make a documentary film of the country. There was a misunderstanding about the size of the films and the Mongolians had locked up his cameras, didn't allow him to move, and put him, his men and equipment on the first plane out to Moscow and he was on his way back to the United States. That wasn't very encouraging to us. All this time our nurse-teacher (reminding me of Nurse Jane Fuzzy Wuzzy in *Uncle Wiggley*) was in evidence, keeping track of us as if we were school children on a class trip to a museum or a strange city.

By the time the plane came in we were really weary, and we were cold, which I didn't mind after all the heat we have been in. My feet were swollen and H. said his were too, but at least his didn't show. I was now resigned to whatever happened in Mongolia and I was so tired I didn't care.

The stewardess on the plane to Ulan Bator was Mongolian and wore the Mongolian dress. She had her hair in braids and looked just like some of the women we had met in Sikkim. She gave us a snack of a fruit drink and those delicious Russian chocolate candies that are more like cookies, Myilki, or Three Bears. From this plane we could see a lot of the country below us and if I hadn't known where we were I think I would have guessed it was Mongolia. It looks just the way it does in pictures, and just the way I have always thought of it; lovely smooth plains and gentle mountains surrounding them, all a soft green. As we came down we could see clusters of white gers, or yurts, the round tents which are homes for all the Mongolians who don't live in the city.

At the airport no one met us, either to welcome us or kick us out, in fact no one paid any attention to us at all; we might have been getting off a plane at Hartford. A mod-looking boy, who was returning from studying in Bulgaria and who spoke Russian, came to our assistance and finally we located an Intourist man. He arrived with a car, piled us into it and brought us here to the hotel where we were quickly taken up to a suite of bedroom, living room and bath. It was not very pretty but the bed looked so puffy and inviting I could hardly wait to get into it. Harrison had just brushed his teeth and I was about to brush mine—the first step towards feeling normal again after our thirty-six hours of travelling—when several men appeared and announced that we were to move to a different suite two floors down. I was so relieved they were not policemen to take us off to jail I would have done anything they suggested. The new suite was bigger and more elaborate and in the front with a wonderful view of the mountains.

So we settled in a bit; it was then about six o'clock Saturday, Ulan Bator time. Thank heaven I hadn't sent my wool suit home. I put it on, plus two sweaters and my raincoat, and we went out for a walk.

Though there are mountains all around, and hills on the way in from the airport, this part of the city is flat. The streets are wide and there are newly-planted trees everywhere. The square is enormous, perfect for parades and drills and public gatherings, with a statue of Sukhe Bator, the hero of the 1921 uprising, in the middle, public buildings on three sides and a park and street going out and down to the river on the other. I was surprised to see a statue of

Stalin in front of the library—I thought they had all been removed. We dined early and slept from nine to nine. Rarely have I been so exhausted and it was much worse for H. as in addition to the travelling and waiting around, he was actually talking to and trying to deal with the unbending absolute of Communist bureaucracy for six hours straight.

This morning we met Owen Lattimore and joined him at his table for breakfast. This threw the whole dining room staff into a panic. First they said we had to pay cash for our meals; we said we had signed for dinner the night before and expected to sign for all our meals while at the hotel. Then they said that the girl who adds up the slips, or works the machine to add them, wasn't there. Finally they said it was because we weren't sitting at the table which had been assigned to us. So Professor Lattimore, who is loved and trusted by all the Mongolians, is coming to sit at our table and then it will be o.k. for us to sign the slips.

The next crisis was the eggs. As in Irkutsk, one order of eggs means three eggs whether poached or boiled or fried. I just don't want three eggs for breakfast and I can't bear to leave two uneaten on my plate but it was impossible to explain. So Harrison ordered eggs for himself and gave me one, which satisfied him, me and the waitress. Kumis is a popular drink here; it is fermented mare's milk and I don't like it at all in spite of H. and Professor Lattimore telling me how wonderful and pure and healthy it is. It is too sharp and acidy. It is also supposed to have a mild kick but there are other more pleasant ways to get a little tight.

The British Ambassador and his wife live in this hotel, as does the French (so far only the Communist countries seem to have embassies and houses of their own) and we went up to have tea with them. Like so much that is English, afternoon tea is a comfort, especially in a strange country—a restful, civilized custom. We had bread that the ambassador's wife had made in her on-top-of-the-stove oven and strawberry jam and little cakes, and had a good time talking about mutual friends and acquaintances.

As we were returning to our rooms, we saw the manager of the hotel sitting in the upstairs hall waiting for us. With him was a man who looked just like Dr. Fu Manchu with heavy rimmed glasses and a pointed beard, an interpreter. With extreme politeness, they informed us what we already knew—that our visas had expired; we had entered their country without permission under false pretenses; it was a very serious thing; it was impossible to get hold of any government official because this was Sunday, all offices were closed. Monday, Tuesday and Wednesday they would also be closed as it was the national holiday, the Nadam. The manager was very sorry, we would have to stay inside the hotel until an official could be contacted.

Harrison explained what had happened, how we were the victims of rain in Sikkim, the vagueness and inefficiency of the Indian travel agent in Delhi, and the rigidity of the Russians; how we had tried to get our visas extended in India, and when that failed, hoped to in Moscow, how sorry we were, but we really had had no choice when the Russians had sent us on here.

They apologized to us and we apologized to them and here we are. Except for the six hours in the Moscow airport where the officials were not very polite or helpful or considerate in any way, this is my first experience in a Communist country and I think they are being extremely kind to us. They could put us in jail, for instance, and be perfectly justified.

This unfortunate situation made me feel very homesick, especially as today is Curtis' birthday. It is amazing to think he is fifteen and Charlotte is thirty. I remember when he was born she said, "Gosh, Mummy, when Curtis is my age you'll have both feet in the grave." Fifteen more years and it will be thirty for him, forty-five for her and sixty-seven for me, if I last that long.

July 11

WE WERE waked up at six fifteen by a very loud voice followed by music from a loud speaker. It continued on and gradually people, floats, trucks and machinery assembled for the parade. We are fortunate to be in these rooms because while we can't see the square and the reviewing stand, we can see on two sides of the hotel, and the parade seemed to assemble and start from here. It rained, in sheets, as in Sikkim, all day, but everything went off as planned. The athletes in blue tights and next-to-nothing red shirts and the girls in green sleeveless tops and short white pleated skirts, stood for hours while everything and everyone got into the right position, then marched for hours more in the cold, relentless rain. Rugged as they are they looked miserable with their black hair plastered on their heads and water running off their strong arms as they swung them high, striding along to the martial music.

We saw many posters with pictures of Vietnamese men,

women and children and "All hail to our Vietnamese brothers" in huge letters. I was glad I wasn't out there—it is bad enough to be alone and watching demonstrations against my country because I feel it is against me, personally, and I guess it is. I felt again, we have to find some other way of coping with world problems, war only makes it all worse in the end, besides being so cruel and immoral. It seems odd to me that our government is either so blind that it doesn't see or so arrogant that it doesn't care, that this war and our policy has caused all sorts of people to feel the same about us, has united people and countries who might otherwise be enemies of each other.

This enforced seclusion is hard on Harrison. He is very good about it but must be chafing inside. It is sad because he has been here twice before, he loves this country and the people and feels terribly to have caused any misunderstanding. He has sent a letter to the Foreign Office explaining our predicament but we don't know if there will be anyone there to receive it until after the holidays. I feel like a child again, being sent up to my room for being bad. Thank heaven I brought some knitting. I finished one sock and am well along on the second. H. says it is the first sock anyone has ever knitted for him in his life and he is very impressed.

July 12

THIS morning the manager and the interpreter came to say that the Foreign Office wanted to see Harrison and that they would accompany him there. H. told me to stay in the hotel and I must have looked worried for the interpreter said matter-of-factly, "Don't worry, he will come back." For about two hours I waited with my fingers crossed, scarcely daring to hope we could stay. But the thought that we might be put on the next plane out and then where . . . was too grim to contemplate. Finally he returned with the good news that everything was all right; the Mongolians understood our plight; we can stay, our visas are extended to July 21, we can travel around the country. It was such a relief I was stunned, I still can't believe it. Harrison told the man at the Foreign Office that we felt like children being kept in for being naughty while everyone else had gone out to play, and he replied, "Mr. Salisbury, you are supposed to be a serious journalist and commentator, and you are just a joker." We are not sure what we will do after here; neither of us is in the mood for a boat trip, or Japan, but perhaps that will change. After all, we have been in such a state of uncertainty for three weeks now it has affected everything. Maybe a few days of no worry will make us feel differently.

After our release we went out for a walk around the square and when we came back I collapsed; I felt all shaky and peculiar and had to lie down. In about half an hour I felt better so joined H. and Owen at lunch. H. says it was the reaction of being freed. Maybe. When I was lying on my bed I tried to sort out what was wrong. I feel fine every other way so perhaps it was emotional, a combination of the problems about the visas on top of the reaction to Vietnam which we have encountered everywhere. I have never been confined by a government before and I know it was quite a shock. I take everything personally, right inside to my bones, and it was a terrible blow to realize that people don't regard me as a friend, don't want me, or trust me, to be in their country. All along on this trip, everywhere we have been, I have felt the anti-American feeling and have felt guilty and ashamed. No one has been rude or nasty to us, but I have felt it in spite of their manners. What we are doing in Vietnam looks so different from here. I wish every American could see and hear for himself what we have. From America so much can be theory and ideas; in Asia it is actually happening and is real.

It continued to rain hard most of the day and all the scheduled holiday events were called off, including the famous horse race. Children ride a distance of thirty miles in this race and often get so tired they fall asleep towards the end. People ride out to meet them and grab them before they fall off. Late in the afternoon we took another short walk, met the French Ambassador in the lobby afterwards and went up to his room for a visit. The Ambassador has his office in Paris, comes here for two or three weeks every three or four months, then goes to Peking, then back to Paris, thus keeping in touch with what is going on in this part of the world. I keep thinking, what is the matter with the United States, why don't we have ambassadors and representatives in all the countries in the world? What if they are Communists? That is their business. We are so self-righteous and arrogant to think our way is the only way—it is just what we accuse the Communists of thinking in reverse. Maybe democracy is the best for us, but we have no right to push our ideology on others who have different beliefs. Right or wrong, good or evil, black or white—none are the same to Asians as to us. We think we can separate everything, and we try to; they know it can't be done and don't try. A friend told me that the Asian philosophy is to grind up everything together, the bad with the good, and what comes out is life, reality; that's the way it is. It is a pity we can't try to get along with everyone whatever their government is. How much more we would know, how much better able to understand other countries, their people and their governments, their religions and motivations. If I were the president for a while the first thing I would do would be to stop the war in Vietnam. Next I would establish diplomatic relations with every country in the world that would have us, and I'd work to make it all countries so that those that didn't think they wanted us would feel that it would be to their advantage to admit us. We wouldn't have to admire or approve of their policies; we would simply be there learning about them. I would have small efficient embassies and not flood foreign capitals with Americans and so much money that it disrupted their economy. I wonder how many other Americans feel this way. Perhaps they haven't thought about it, but it is so obviously the only way to get along with the rest of the world I can't understand how or why we ever developed the short-sighted policy we have.

July 13

THE storm is a disaster. It has disrupted the electricity and the water pumping station so the city has been without lights or water since yesterday. The telephone, telegraph, radio, are all out; a bridge on the edge of the city is out and the road to the airport is flooded and impassable. Four thousand people are homeless and many children are missing—washed away by the river. It is too horrible to think about. A helicopter is flying back and forth across the river bringing stranded people and landing them in the big square one block from here. Schools are being used as shelters and we see many Red Cross ambulances and cars. It is a sad way to end the national holiday.

We are very fortunate; an army kitchen has moved in to the hotel and so far we have hot meals; we still get hot, boiled water in the morning—kipitok—to make coffee with, and they bring buckets of water for washing, etc. There are many more guests in the hotel than usual, due to the holiday, and heaven knows when anyone will be able to leave.

We now have an interpreter-guide to be with us when we need him, a young man named Darum who has been studying English for three years. Before lunch we took a drive around the city, the first time since our arrival that we have been further than a few blocks from the hotel. Everything is wet, the houses still streaked; bedding, furniture and clothes, all soaked by rain, were on porches and steps, drying out, and there were pools of water in the streets. The most serious damage is where the river surged over its banks and we didn't go down there.

Ulan Bator is a well-planned city, laid out in wide streets and planted with poplars and larch trees. There is plenty of grass and space between the buildings which are simple and neat, stucco over brick, and painted white or light colors, pink, yellow, blue. Some of the embassy houses are pretty with pillars and verandahs and would look just right near the Mediterranean or southern California, or in any of the countries of Southeast Asia which we have been to on this trip. It is odd that they look just right here, too. Two apartment houses of ten or more stories are being built by the Chinese. The workers come in groups, live in camps, keep entirely to themselves and work even on the Mongolian holidays. Many flowers grow in the city, in the park across from our hotel, and in front of the houses, and most of them are familiar—cosmos, English daisies, pansies, and some of the wildflowers we have at home. There is always a vase on every table in the hotel dining room filled with miniature tiger lilies, lupin, a kind of Queen Anne's lace and yarrow. Best to me are the wild pink roses, exactly the same as on Cape Cod.

The people are enchanting. Everyone looks so sturdy, has such rich red cheeks, black, black, hair, and seems ready to smile and laugh at any and everything. The women and girls are terribly pretty and most of them wear their hair done up high. The younger girls have braids and all wear earrings. Both men and women wear a del, which is like the bakku the Sikkimese men wear. It can be made of cotton or silk, and padded or lined with fur when it is cold. It is attractive, becoming, and perfectly suited to the life. The women tie a scarf made of thin, stiff material like tulle or net around their hair-dos to keep them from blowing in the constant wind. The men are strong and solid and sit on their horses, which are as sturdy and solid as the men, as if they were all one piece. It is such a relief to see these round healthy little horses after those in India.

The children are smaller editions of their parents—usually square with clothes and utterly adorable. Babies are swaddled until they cannot bend or be bent. I saw a young father holding his baby, who looked like a big package from the back, kissing the little brown face that emerged at the top. I remarked to Owen Lattimore that I couldn't get over the people, they look so beguiling. He said, "Everyone falls in love with the people."

This afternoon we walked around to see if any stores were open. All seemed to be shut except the big state department store, so we climbed up the four or five flights and leisurely walked down and through each floor. It is a well-stocked store, like a Sears Roebuck in a small city in America. There were souvenirs which are attractive and useful, decorated china cups and bowls, for example; pictures and wood carvings, some cheap, some expensive; all sorts of electric irons, burners, ice boxes, bicycles, cameras and films. We saw a section of plastic cups and utensils that might have been in any American department store or Woolworth's; lots of yard goods, cotton, wool, velvet and silk; underclothes for men, women and children; blouses, shoes, coats—almost anything you can think of except ready-made women's clothes. Either I missed them or they don't carry them as every woman we see wears a del.

The streets were crowded with refugees from the flood, many standing in long lines waiting for food, others sitting in the street on and around their belongings which usually were wrapped up in a piece of material. A mother had undressed her little girl of about three and was trying to find something dry from just such a bundle to put on her child. Like all people in situations where they have no control, they were just sitting, waiting. Army trucks were bringing in survivors from this side of the raging Tola river and two helicopters flew back and forth rescuing those on the other side who had escaped being swept away but had lost everything and could not get across the river. We are told the Russians have sent all kinds of assistance and many of the trucks and the helicopters are Russian, but the Chinese seem to be ignoring both the holiday and the flood.

As we were walking home there was a terrible clap of thunder. The sky was a beautiful, dark grey, lovely with the pink buildings, but ominous, and before we had progressed very far the skies opened and the rain came down in sheets and floods. We stopped for a bit under a shelter in the park but we were already so wet we soon went on. Crossing the street was like fording a river and I had to hold on to Harrison's hand to feel at all safe. Back at the hotel we changed our clothes and the sun came out, but there is still no electricity and no water, which seems so absurd in a flood.

July 14

LAST night the lights, which were provided by an army generator, were on dimly for a while, but this morning the important Russian and Chinese guests left and the word is we won't have any light tonight. They say there won't be any water until August first, or later. Not only are all the generating and power plants under water, but a lot of the equipment has been washed away. It is a major catastrophe and we are told that the government has made a world-wide appeal for help.

Today was bright and beautiful and it seems impossible we are in the same city as the one we have seen for the last two days. We visited the museum and saw fine exhibits of animals (wolves, tigers, many kinds of deer, the wild horses), archaeological findings of dinosaurs and early civilizations, a big collection of pictures and data about the 1921 revolution, a wonderful collection of clothes and a model of a yurt. The yurt was much more substantial than I had imagined. It was furnished with beds, tables, chests of drawers, low sofa-beds around the sides and beautiful rugs and it wasn't anything like a tent. We drove as near as we could, then walked, to the river to see how far it has run over; it is terrifying, still surging and tearing through part of the city, still way over its banks. Helicopters are still flying back and forth over it, looking for survivors, and, like the trucks, are still bringing families who have lost everything into the city.

Late this afternoon the French Ambassador had a reception to celebrate Bastille Day. As there is no ice, all the drinks were warm, including the otherwise perfect French champagne. The guests included all the embassy people from Russia, China, North Vietnam, Hungary, Bulgaria, Rumania, Czechoslovakia, East Germany, Cuba—all Communist countries—and prominent Mongolians who could take a minute off from their struggles with the flood damage. We were introduced to everyone except the Chinese and the North Vietnamese. I was very proud of the English ambassador and his wife, and of our host and of Professor Lattimore, who now lives in England, and I wished again that we had a government representative here. One man would do. That's all the French have and his secretary is a Frenchwoman who works in the French Embassy in Peking when she isn't here. She had lived there many years ago and was curious to see what it is like now so got herself assigned to a tour of duty there for a while. If we had just a toe in the door, even a tentative contact, we would have at least some hope for understanding other people, but if we refuse to have anything to do with them because they are different, and think differently than we do, then there is no hope. And we will be the losers in the end. There are many more of all these other people than there are of us, Americans, which is something we should begin to think about, just to be practical.

July 16

Two more days and still there is no water and only very dim light intermittently from the portable generators. We are getting used to this way of living but it's not very attractive and the hotel is smelly at times. People don't open the windows in this part of the world the way I was brought up to and when no one is around I open the one in the hall near our room, but it is always closed the next time I'm out there. We haven't had kipitok for two mornings but the bathtub is kept filled with slightly muddy water for our other needs. It is carried up from the river. The food seems just the same as before the flood. We have eggs cooked any way we want, tea, bread, some strange meat dishes and as much rice as at first. The Mongolians don't eat vegetables and fruit the way we do; the only vegetables are pale tomatoes and cucumbers grown under glass, and occasionally for dessert I have three tiny pieces of dried apple floating in a watery syrup. I imagine that a people who for centuries have roamed the plains and lived in houses they can dismantle in minutes have never had the inclination or the need to cultivate the soil.

Every morning I have been waked up at six by a program from the Ulan Bator radio station which somehow still is working. It is broadcast out of a loudspeaker directly into our windows from across the park and right into my only hearing ear, or so it seems. First there are bells for about fifteen minutes, then the national anthem, then news announcements and several other talks, none of which I understand. Then more music and the program is ended at six thirty-five when I am so thoroughly awake I can't possibly go back to sleep, though Harrison, when he does wake up, like this morning, can. He is amazing, he can sleep through anything and go to sleep anywhere at any time. I have become so conditioned to this program that this morning I was wide awake promptly at six, waiting for the bells, but the program manager must have overslept for they were omitted today; the national anthem started off the day at six fifteen. Unfortunately one can't turn off this all-over-the-city broadcasting that can be heard even behind closed windows and doors. I believe it is prevalent in Communist countries. The musak we have in elevators and airplanes and other public places demands the same kind of forced listening, but at least we don't have to listen to a lot of government propaganda. That would be unbearable, especially now.

In these last two days we have seen about as much as can be seen here in the city. Because of the flood we can't go anywhere else, not to the Gobi desert, which we had hoped to see, or to Erdeni Dzuu, the Buddhist monastery built on the site of Karakorum, capital city of Genghis Khan. There is so much history here, as in all of Asia. It is too bad we can't see more of the old Mongolia. Ulan Bator is a city we might find in any country which is trying to throw off their more primitive customs and get into the swing of the twentieth century. Speaking of swing, we have been amused at the young Mongolians, the same as the young anywhere, in tight pants and short skirts (forsaking the del) hanging around the huge juke box at one end of the dining room listening to recordings by the Beatles, the Rolling Stones, Petula Clark and other Western singers. The juke box comes from East Germany.

We visited the Old Monastery which is now a museum. It has been kept the same as when it was an active working monastery and is very like the monasteries in Sikkim. Pictures of horses and landscapes and beguiling sculptures of ponies and deer show its relation to life here in Mongolia as well as to Buddha.

Gandang is the only monastery where there are services. We were there during one and heard the familiar chanting of the monks. A few believers prayed in and outside of the temple and women were giving matches and other offerings to the monks. We had tea with the head abbot, sitting in his yurt, which is richly furnished with red and gold painted furniture and beautiful rugs. (The tea is five elements tea, consisting of tea, water, butter, salt and milk. We had this in Sikkim, too.) The abbot told us that the government doesn't interfere with them and that there are more monks now in Mongolia than a few years ago, but I believe Gandang is the only functioning monastery in the whole country. We also have been to the university and Harrison talked with the head, or president, who is an old friend from his previous trips to Mongolia.

To celebrate the Nadam, entertainers from ten Communist countries have been here since Sunday, waiting impatiently to put on their show. The electricity was on yesterday evening and the show was scheduled for eight last night in the opera house, a big orange building with white columns on one side of the square. Inside it is a pretty shape with a curving balcony and decorated like Carnegie Hall in white, red and gold. It was packed; every seat was taken and people stood in back and along the sides, eagerly waiting for the entertainment the actors had travelled so far to bring them. After the trials of the past three days it was almost magic to be going to the theatre.

First there was a Mongolian herdsman dance that was reminiscent of the Russian Moiseyev dances, very fast and gay, followed by singers and dancers from Poland and Yugoslavia. All sang strictly native songs and wore the costumes of their own country except for a Yugoslavian blues singer who might have been singing in a Paris or New York night club. She brought down the house. Next was a Hungarian man we had met at the French Ambassador's reception. His voice is deep and pure and he sang to a piano accompaniment played by a beautiful, exquisitely coiffed blonde in a tight black dress who looked like Eva Gabor. In the middle of his second song the lights flickered and went out. He valiantly finished in the dark, the audience applauded, and we sat back, accepting the situation as if it had been announced in the program. Darum came down from where he was sitting with friends to tell us the lights would go on again in about ten minutes. We waited over forty-five minutes, gave up, stumbled out of the pitch black house and walked home. All the actors were standing out back of the theatre, smoking and discussing what to do. I wondered why they didn't get some candles and a lantern and light up the stage a bit and finish what they could of the show. But either there were no candles or no one thought of it.

The lights were out for two and a half hours; the

audience sat waiting patiently in the dark the entire time but all the performers gave up and went to bed. When the lights finally came on, the Mongolians went over to the hotel, woke up the actors, saying, "The lights are on, the audience is still there, get up and come over and finish the performance." So over they went, the show was resumed and it wasn't over until well after two a.m. Our friend sang Ol' Man River, "Just for you," he said to us. I wish we had heard him; his voice is perfect for the song.

This afternoon H. saw the foreign minister and I packed. We have been able to get transit visas for Siberia so our plans are to go to Irkutsk for two days and see what we can arrange from there. We still have our tickets for the boat to Japan and we are beginning to think we would like to go that way after all. Though we are not leaving until Monday morning, we were told to take our suitcases out to the airport, go through customs and have our tickets checked because Sunday is a holiday and the personnel might not be there on Monday. So we kept out enough to wear and complied, leaving our bags out there. The English Ambassador told us the reason for this is to have the paper work done and on the records—we could have brought our bags back, but we weren't aware of that. Such strange ways of doing things. When we drove to the airport we saw some of the flood damage we hadn't seen before; railroad tracks washed out, lumber from a saw mill swept out of the yards and great logs piled up like jackstraws or toothpicks; factories with water still in the ground floor, and hundreds of yurts, or gers, put up on the hills by families lucky enough not to have had their houses swept away in the rushing river. There were two large areas of gers and a steady stream of trucks arriving, heaped with whatever could be rescued or salvaged, and the bedraggled survivors sitting on top. Even when a household is properly packed and moved by a professional mover, one's belongings have a way of looking much shabbier and sadder than when in place in a house, but the remnants of any household after a disaster like a fire or flood are pitiful. These were no exception. The only good thing was that in many cases they could bring their houses with them.

July 17

THIS morning we watched the preliminary rounds of wrestling and a big parade of all the youth, athletes and acrobats. These events took place in an arena on the eastern outskirts of the city as the stadium is still under water. I believe the wrestling is unique to Mongolia. The object is for one man to force the other to touch the ground with some part of his body other than his feet. The opponents spar around at first and usually get into a clinch with their arms; then it is a question of who has superior strength to twist the other over to the ground. It can be quick and active but more often they get locked together and stay looking like a human staple for a long time until one gives a little; then the other quickly takes advantage and hurls him down. The winner dances toward the onlookers in a strange slow-motion hopping movement, waving his arms over his head, a ritual representing the walk of an eagle and is wildly applauded. We were going to see the finals this afternoon but first there was a big dust storm, then terrible wind and a thunderstorm with rain and hail battering this poor city again, so they are postponed.

Life is slowly moving back to normal; the loudspeaker in the street has been turned off at last; we have had electricity off and on ever since the relief generator was brought in, and there has been running water at two separate times this afternoon, why or how no one seems to fathom. Looking at the twenty-five hundred students marching, plus twenty thousand spectators in the arena this morning, I couldn't help but think—all these people and not a toilet working in the entire city. It's a wonder everyone hasn't got cholera and typhoid. Harrison says he thinks the flood will put the Mongols back a year at least in their plans for modernizing their country. I keep thinking of the flood in Connecticut in 1956; it took months for life to pick up and get back to normal and there are still many signs of the destruction and damage.

Harrison had a big row with the cashier because the bill was much bigger than they had said it would be, and he refused to break down the costs. The manager with whom we have had so many friendly dealings was not available (he ceremoniously came to say goodby on Saturday, saying he had to be away for a few days, but we saw him at the wrestling this morning and I wonder if there was a method in his actions) and there was no one else to discuss it with. It was upsetting to H. and leaves a bad taste.

July 18, On the plane to Irkutsk

WE LEFT at eight, with Owen and the English Ambassador and his wife waving goodby from the hotel steps. Darum was dressed in country clothes, a raincoat and beret, very different from his usual city clothes, and he said he had just had word his mother is sick so he is going two hundred kilometers to see her. A friend with a motorcycle was to take him and the friend followed us out to the airport so they could start as soon as we left. About a mile from the airport a car was stopped on the side of the road and two men, a woman and a boy were waving wildly. We stopped and before we had time to ask them what they wanted or offer them a ride one man jumped on behind Darum's friend on the motorcycle, the others squashed into our car with an air of great urgency, and we dashed on to the airport. They were Russian; the woman's brother had died suddenly at age twenty-seven and they were hurrying to Moscow. Several cars had passed them without stopping and they had been frantic for fear they would miss the only plane out for three more days.

We got on this plane only after the most thorough search of our hand luggage, even my pocket book, for films. The flight is pleasant and the country beautiful to look at but I am glad to be leaving Mongolia. Sometime, if it would be possible to move around more and see some of the country, I would like to come here again, but not to just stay in Ulan Bator. However, the flood and ensuing problems made everything either difficult or impossible and I do think the hotel did a remarkable job of feeding and somehow taking care of all the guests staying there. And, except for the cashier cheating us and the manager deserting us, we liked the people.

☲ eight

July 18, 6 p.m. Hotel Siberia, Irkutsk

EVERYTHNG is so lovely I can hardly believe it. Intourist has taken complete charge of us; we have a nice room and bath in this comfortable, if not very attractive, hotel, and will stay two nights here. We will fly to Khabarovsk for two more days, take the Trans-Siberian overnight to Nakhodka and from there go by boat to Yokohama. All our tickets are in order; everyone is terribly pleasant; we had a wonderful lunch; a lovely young girl is our guide here and took us on a tour of the city; I have washed a lot of our clothes; we have each had a good hot bath; you can drink the water from the tap; we are going to the opera tonight to hear *Traviata* and will have dinner at eleven p.m. Quite a different life from the last week.

At the airport here this morning the customs official, a

young blonde woman, asked, "Have you anything from Pe-king. . . I mean Mongolia?" When we told her we had only papers which Mongolian officials had given Harrison, she nodded and closed up our bags. H. says the atmosphere is so different from the first time he went to Mongolia in 1959. At that time he flew in a Russian-built, Chinese airline plane manned by a Chinese crew. Most of the passengers were Chinese and they got preferred treatment while H. was looked at with suspicion. In 1962, as now, the plane was Russian-built, but Mongolian-owned with Mongolian per-sonnel. Any Chinese travellers and their luggage were searched carefully for offending documents. Today we were regarded as friends and there were no Chinese travel-lers, no Chinese planes and no Chinese personnel.

July 19

HEARING an Italian opera sung in Russian by Bur-yat-Mongolian singers in an opera house in Siberia is an experience I don't believe many Americans have had, and we enjoyed it so much we went again tonight to hear *Faust*. Violetta was pretty and her voice was pleasant and ade-quate; Alfredo was terrible, we thought, but he was popular with the audience; his father was the star, by far the best in every way. Unfortunately the performance this evening did not live up to last night's, at least for us. Alfredo played Faust and wasn't any better than in his previous role; Mar-guerite wasn't very appealing so in spite of Alfredo's father who, as Mephistopheles, again was the star, we left. Strange-ly the house was full tonight while last night more than half the seats were empty. We were impressed at how many young boys and girls were in the audience both nights.

This morning at ten we drove with Sonya, our guide, to Lake Baikal. It is about seventy kilometers from here and our car barely touched the ground all the way; we got there in no time at all. The road was full of women and children walking, people on bicycles, trucks and other cars, road repair men and construction machinery, but nothing slowed us down. I said to H. that if there were any question about the other traffic or the condition of the road or whether to pass or not, the solution seemed to be to simply go faster. It was a beautiful day, the sun was shining in a bright, blue sky, the woods were wonderfully green, the fields and road-sides were covered with wildflowers and Sonya was singing away in the front seat next to the driver. So we hung on to the sides of the car and to each other and abandoned our-selves to the spirit. We should have been in an open sleigh or wagon, singing and drinking and throwing bottles out all over the place.

Our first stop was the museum where we saw exhibits of the wild life and minerals, and maps and pictures telling the history of the lake. We learned that it is the largest and deepest body of fresh water in the world and is nearly four hundred miles long and over forty miles wide at one place. There are over one thousand different kinds of fish and animals and many plants not found anywhere else in the world. The water is still absolutely pure; there is no pollu-tion. But a paper mill is being built, is nearly finished, and, when operating, will discharge its industrial waste into the lake; any other method of disposing of it is too expensive. A guide at the museum told us that, once polluted, over four hundred years would have to pass before the water would be clean again. In Russia and all over the world, conservationists have been deploring this and are fighting it. But it seems universal; business and industry, no matter how irresponsible, seem to win out, even in a Communist country. When will people learn that nature can't be abused so—that we can't pour refuse into the air and water and still have any life or health in either? Already there is little water left that is clean and the air in most cities is dangerously laden with smog, soot and fumes. Many vegetables and fruits have no value in them because the soil they grow in is so sterile and some foods have preservatives and coloring that are poisonous; grains and sugar are so refined that they are useless as well as tasteless. Because of the indiscriminate use of chemical sprays, butterflies all over the world have decreased substantially and many pests that were wiped out for several years are now back, bigger and stronger than ever and impervious to the chemicals that subdued them temporarily, but destroyed for good are more delicate species. So now the whole balance is off and what next? A friend of ours is always quoting, "Whom the Gods would destroy, they first make mad," and that seems to be applicable to our world. Even discounting war we are doing our best to make the earth uninhabitable.

We drove up to the top of a high hill and had a view for miles of Lake Baikal. There were mountains all around the edge as far as we could see and it is so deep the water looks gray or black. But where it flows out and becomes the Angara river it is a beautiful, deep, sapphire blue. We sat on the rocks, listening to the wind in the pine trees, breathing the clear, clean air and letting the sun warm us through. We might have been in the Adirondacks in the fall or in parts of Wyoming or Montana. There are wildflowers everywhere and almost all are the same as we have at home. Every kind is out at once: daisies, dandelions, buttercups, mustard, Queen Anne's lace, white and mauve yarrow, and flowers that looked like steeplebush, roadside phlox and a type of bee balm—all growing in profusion wherever there was sun and an open place in the forests and all over the fields and roadsides. In the village down beside the lake where we had lunch the lilacs were blooming, five weeks later than the lilacs had bloomed in Irkutsk. In Siberia, as in so many parts of Europe, wildflowers are picked and sold in great bunches on street corners in the city and yet there are always quantities growing over the countryside.

For lunch we had the special fish of this area—Omul— first in a soup, then fried. It is an awfully good, delicate, white fish. The meal began, as usual, with caviar. We are getting very spoiled here. I can't imagine having fresh caviar twice a day in New York; once a year when a friend sends us some we feel blessed. We came back to the city by hydrofoil—the first time either H. or I had been in one. We skimmed the water like a sea gull but it didn't seem any more like flying than our morning ride out in the car.

Back here we tried for the second time to get inside a church but, as yesterday, it was locked up tight. On the outside it was very pretty, white stucco with green trim. The small wood houses, in the city and out by the lake, are typical of Siberia. Usually only one story, they have lovely carving around the windows and on the doors and shutters. Most are dark brown but a few are painted pale blue or yellow. Always there are flowers on the sills inside; in fact there are flowers everywhere, in jars on top of piles of canned goods in a grocery store or in a tin at an ice cream stand on a street corner. Irkutsk is an old city; it has been and is now the center of culture for much of Siberia. There are parks and schools, shops and theatres and industry. There are lovely old trees on the wide streets and we noticed that in all the recently built areas of this expanding city double rows of young trees have been planted. I have been fascinated to notice that all the telephones in the hotel are bright colored. The one in our room is emerald green.

July 20, *On the plane to Khabarovsk*

SONYA picked us up around nine at the hotel and brought us to the airport where she turned us over to an official airport lady who immediately led us to this plane. There was no fuss about our tickets or passports or papers, or any of the irritating petty problems we are now so used to. When Intourist wants to make travel and sightseeing pleasant they certainly can do it. We had a perfect stay in Irkutsk and we loved our guide.

We were escorted straight to our seats and the plane gradually filled up with passengers, all Russian. All the time one poor woman, by herself, was taking away from the cabin kitchenette large, empty, metal containers and bringing in full ones. Another woman was sweeping under the seats. I wonder why they don't do all that first before any passengers get on. That way it would take half the time. Finally everything was ready and we sat in the broiling sun for about thirty-five minutes. In some parts of Russia, and other countries we've flown in, planes are towed by trucks to the take-off strip and the ventilating system isn't turned on until the engines start. A few passengers began to won-

der about the delay and asked the reason why. At last the
pilot walked grandly through the plane, someone said,
"Here's the chauffeur, now we can start," and off we went,
one hour late.

July 21, Khabarovsk

THE passengers on the plane yesterday were a jolly
group; during the initial delay they had been making jokes
and laughing with each other and later during the flight,
when the rumor spread that we were landing at Vladivostok
instead of Khabarovsk, there was more joking and specu-
lating; that the pilot didn't feel well, he had a hangover, or
had a girl at Vladivostok, etc. It turned out that there were
severe thunderstorms at Khabarovsk (the reason for the
initial delay at Irkutsk) and it would be impossible to land.
So we went south and came down in Vladivostok. The
officer in charge of the airport met us and led us to a
lounge. There is no Intourist there as Vladivostok is a
closed city now for security reasons and there is no
travelling in or out or it. (We noticed many army planes
lined up on the airfield). It is no longer the big port of Siberia; Nakhodka has taken its place. Obviously our airplane
personnel had informed the officer that we were Intourist
passengers and he treated us with great care and consideration.

The airport was crammed with other travellers stranded
by the storm, over three hundred adults and many children.
It was hot out and hotter in, and very smelly, naturally. But
here, as in Mongolia, no one had thought of opening a door

or window and it was heavy and unpleasant. So we elected to sit in the broiling sun and the officer sat with us. From time to time a man would come and report to him about the weather conditions and there were announcements over the loudspeaker about more delays and what hopes there were, if any, for passengers to be able to resume their travels.

After an hour or so more, there was word we could go around nine p.m. but our companion said we should eat first. Again he led us upstairs, this time through the public restaurant to a special dining room painted brilliant yellow and purple and stifling in the late afternoon sun. We ordered okrushka, a wonderful cold soup, ice cream and vodka. I had never seen a Russian drink before, bottoms up each time, and I was full of admiration for our new friend. I was also full of admiration for myself for getting out of there on my feet; although I didn't match him drink for drink, as he had suggested, I had consumed plenty, and the combination of heat and vodka was potent.

Again we were escorted to a waiting plane and after we were in our seats the other passengers boarded. Every seat was filled by an adult and most of them had children or babies on their laps. While we had waited about three hours, most of these people had been waiting nearly all day at Vladivostok; there were three plane loads heading for Khabarovsk and as we were starting the stewardess announced, "In a few minutes we will be taking off for Vladivostok," which caused great merriment.

The flight took an hour—one of the longest hours of my life, and we skirted and dodged thunderstorms continually. It was spectacular and beautiful in a terrifying way. Black clouds stood out like fierce dragons against the red light from the vanished sun in the west. We were flying right up along the Ussuri river on the Chinese border and it seemed quite natural for it to look so menacing. This was the first time I have been scared in all the flying we have done and it was not because of lack of trust in the pilot or worry that we would be shot at if we flew over China's borders, but because of the lightning. Inside the plane we could hear the thunder crack around us and great streaks of lightning flashed first on one side of the plane then on the other. It was a relief to land and find another pretty Intourist girl waiting for us; she had been expecting us for six hours.

After arriving at the hotel last night we decided a snack before going to bed would be soothing and we had noticed a sign on the door to the restaurant in the lobby saying open from eleven to eleven. It was about ten minutes to eleven but we found the door was shut and locked and the special Intourist dining room was also locked up tight. The doorman realized our predicament, came over and rattled the restaurant doors until I thought they would break. A hand pushed back the curtains behind the doors and a very bleached blonde head appeared and motioned *No* emphatically. The doorman continued his rattling until another cross face appeared conveying the same message. This incensed the doorman who muttered about foreign visitors and went off to get the Intourist man, who got the manager of the hotel, who made the manager of the restaurant open the doors and let us in. It wasn't worth it except for the moral victory; everything we wanted they said they were out of so finally I had cucumbers and more vodka.

This morning we waited until eleven, then went to the public part of the restaurant, not to the special Intourist diningroom, and attempted to order breakfast. We wanted some eggs and asked for them boiled, but the waitress said, no, there were no boiled eggs. Then we asked if we could have some fried, and again she said no, they didn't serve eggs, there weren't any. H. showed surprise but she stuck to her guns—no eggs. We saw omelette listed on the menu and asked if that were available. "Oh, yes?" she said, we could have omelettes. We each ordered one and while not the best in the world, they were not bad either, and were certainly made of real eggs. We had bread, not toast, coffee with hot milk and delicious strawberry jam and tomato juice besides the omelette. The meal took about one hour and fifteen minutes, start to finish.

This hotel is not at all in the same class as the Hotel Siberia in Irkutsk. We have a "suite" of two minute rooms and an awful bathroom. In the bedroom there are two beds placed against the walls at right angles, two tiny stands, one lamp and two chairs, leaving just enough room to get in and out of bed. There are two oriental-type rugs, but they are under the beds, only the edges show. They will last a long time as not even an inch gets walked on.

The living room isn't much bigger and it has a large wardrobe on one wall and an equally large cabinet on the other. The cabinet has drawers and cupboards, two glass shelves with sliding glass doors holding a decanter and six vodka glasses, two cut glass vases and a high candy dish. Also there is a desk and chair, a table shaped like a heart and two armchairs, a cupboard and a television set. The rug in this room is not as good as the bedroom rugs and it gets walked on. With our four bags and three pieces of hand luggage plus ourselves, it is more like being crammed into a train compartment than being in a hotel suite. The bathroom is very shabby with tiles missing and pipes showing and the water is dirty, but everything works.

Here again we are lucky and have a wonderful, charming man as our guide. We talk about everything with him and feel as if we had known him for years. At one o'clock after our breakfast, Ivan took us for a long drive in and around the city. Harrison had told me that when he was here in 1954 it was the headquarters for the secret police. Everywhere there was forced labor, in the mines, in the lumber camps and right here in the city, men and women working on the buildings we see now, with armed guards posted at every site. There certainly is none of that atmosphere today. The city seems like one of our western cities, young and booming and expanding in every way with new factories, industrial plants, new housing, new streets. The streets are lined with trees and as soon as any building or street is finished new young trees are planted. A beach runs along the river and a marina harbors small boats which are used for fishing or pleasure trips on the river, maybe toward China. On the flight from Vladivostok and here, as in all the places we have been to which lie so near to her borders, I feel the fear that permeates the regions close to China, fear of a giant watching, waiting for the right moment to reach out for more land, more food, more resources.

On the outskirts of the city there are colonies of dachas whose owners live in apartments during the week and go to their dachas over weekends and in the summer, the way so many city-dwelling Americans do. The difference is the size. Here a two-room apartment is above average for a family of four and the dachas are small old-fashioned cottages, usually one story and a pointed peaked roof.

Some look like the gingerbread house in *Hansel and Gretel*. Each has a small garden plot for berries and vegetables; each has its own outhouse. There are wells—one for a number of families, and the water is carried to the houses. Older people who have retired and live on pensions usually live in their dacha all the year round. As more and more Russians are moving to the city to work, the week-end and summer place, no matter how small or primitive, where a family can be in the country and grow a lot of their food, is becoming a vital part of the social set-up.

We visited a cement factory where sections are made for apartment houses, schools and all kinds of buildings. There were linings for wells, coverings for huge pipes and almost anything you could think of to do with building. The sections of walls for apartment houses have double casement windows all set in, complete with the glass. I should think they would break in shipping but evidently they don't.

We also went to the Medical Institute, which is on the square across from our hotel, and met the doctors in charge. Unfortunately this is vacation, so there were no students and no classes. But we had a tour of the buildings and saw the classrooms and laboratories full of equipment and specimens. A chic, well-dressed, good-looking woman with black hair was our guide. She spoke English perfectly. Of course, with Harrison speaking Russian I never have to worry, but it is nice when I can communicate directly with a person as with Sonya and Ivan. Their medical school is about like ours; the course takes six years which I believe corresponds to our four years of school and two of interning. They have more women than men in training and, as we have seen, there are many women doctors in the Soviet Union.

We were going to the ballet at seven so we decided we

must leave plenty of time for supper. At a quarter of five we sat down in the dining room and ordered soup, salad and dessert. This meal took one and a half hours. Ivan came with us and we saw "The Stone Flower," performed by the Novosibirsk Company which is on tour. The dancers were their third string but they were excellent. The theatre was large and every seat was taken. Before this trip whenever I thought of Siberia I certainly never thought of grand opera and ballet. Everything here has been a surprise to me, especially the beauty and the feeling of familiarity with the country and the people. I feel so much at home. Everyone we have met is so friendly and so direct. Over and over again I am reminded of the refreshing easy way of life in our West.

July 22, 4 p.m. Waiting to go to the train.

THIS morning we went upstairs to the hotel "snack bar" and in about ten minutes had a good breakfast of tea and raisin muffins. Ivan took us to the museum and we saw the collection of animals, including a tiger whose habitat is only one hour from here. It seems unbelievable that such a truly wild animal lives so near civilization. These tigers are large and stalwart as well as being graceful and are now protected by law. There were also life-sized models of a house, boots, clothes and utensils, all made and used by tribes who came from here and further north. The beaded work and leather garments were just the same as the American Indian made and wore, as were the household utensils.

This morning, while Harrison was buying books, I found

myself in a section of the store which was given over to the war in Vietnam. A long table was piled with books and on the wall behind were posters. The majority of the books were in Russian but there were a few in English and French and several in languages I didn't recognize, and there were many books of photographs. I opened one of these and saw a picture of a little girl on crutches; both of her legs, one arm and her head were bandaged. Next was a man weeping over what must have been his son's pitiful belongings—a picture, a medal, a knife, some coins. There were pictures of civilians, more of children hit by bombs and then a picture as terrible as any I ever saw of two American soldiers leaning on their guns, looking casually, as if they were looking at the day's duck shooting, at a collection of Vietnamese corpses, torn and mangled and bloody. That human beings can look at the dead bodies of their fellow men no matter who they are or what they have done, with the callous, almost bored, expressions on those two young faces is a shocking commentary on our current state of mind—lacking any heart or pity or compassion.

I was overcome with horror and shock; not that I don't know that this is what is happening, but to see such proof and to realize that it is my country and my government which is causing such destruction and misery is almost too much to bear. Two women had been looking at me—heaven knows what they were thinking—and I couldn't look at them. I closed the book and went out into the street.

Looking back over this long trip, there is this one prevailing thought—we have to stop this war. No matter all the new things I have seen, the new places we have been or what we have done, everything fades away and I can think only of this war. In the advanced state of civilization and technology which we have achieved today if we can't find any better way to solve the problems that beset mankind than to drop bombs on other people's cities, maim their children, wreck their country, and at the same time turn our own young men into either corpses or tough and callous veterans crippled in mind or body or both, then we don't deserve to inherit the earth. The meek are supposed to do that. I have become more and more convinced as the time has gone by that nothing else matters, and it is getting late. Already the majority of world opinion is against us. Most Americans don't realize this. How can they? I never would have felt so strongly unless I had had the chance to make this trip half way around the world and hear what the people who live in this part of it think. What can we do?

July 23, On Trans-Siberian Railroad 9 a.m.

"To THE Pacific Ocean" said the signs on the cars and we waved goodby to Ivan with mingled feelings of anticipation over the next part of our trip and sorrow at leaving our new friend. Though our contact had been brief and, actually, professional, we feel so drawn to him and close in many ways. There was a real sympathy flowing between us. He wants the same things out of life that we do, likes the books that we like, enjoys the same sort of things and has a wonderful sense of humor. Even with their different background the Russians I have talked to out here seem more like Americans than any of the people we have met so far.

We left on the dot of 6:15. This is a lovely comfortable train. We have two berths, an armchair and a table in our compartment; we share a wash basin with a Japanese man in the next compartment and we use the public toilets at each end of the car. A pretty girl is our stewardess and she brought us tea when we woke up this morning. Many of the passengers are Japanese. We have had two delicious meals and are waiting now for our arrival at Nakhodka, in about one hour. Looking out the train windows, we might be travelling in New England. The countryside looks intimate and personal, nothing is vast. There are small settlements, small houses, small ploughed fields, everything on a lesser scale than you would imagine in Siberia.

July 24, On board S.S. Khabarovsk

WE ARRIVED at Nakhodka yesterday morning at exactly 9:55, the scheduled time, went through customs, got our steamship tickets, boarded this ship and sailed at 12:15 precisely. Public transport runs on time in the Soviet Union. The only time we have been delayed was taking off at Irkutsk last Wednesday and that was due to the weather.

Nakhodka is an enormous series of harbors surrounded by hills and sharp mountainous peaks rising up out of the water. Because of the Japanese current it never freezes over, as Vladivostok does. There were freighters from many countries, mostly Japanese, but I didn't notice any United States ships. There were no warships in evidence either.

There are about eighty passengers on this ship. Most are Japanese, some Russian; there are many students and young people from Italy, France and Holland, and a group from the Experiment in International Living. We are the only Americans. The Chilean Ambassador to Moscow, who was in our car on the train, is aboard. He told H. he has eight children, the youngest four stayed behind in Moscow, and this trip with the four older is his vacation. Not many people would consider nine days on a train with four children a holiday and we noticed that Madame spent a lot of the time resting, but this family seems to be having a wonderful time. They are always laughing and talking a blue streak and at meals are especially jolly. There is a young Japanese mother with her daughter and son, aged about six and four. All three are minute and delicate and lovely. I have never had any contact with the Japanese—I only have the prejudices that sprang from the war. I wonder how I will feel when I am in Japan.

Our cabin has a real window which opens onto the promenade deck. It is tiny but comfortable. We sit in the dining room with a young West German engineering student on his way to visit his parents in Japan (his father is an Evangelical Lutheran minister) and a French student who came all the way from Moscow on the train and plans to visit Japan for a month. He is very charming and asks so many questions we imagine all sorts of exciting roles he may be playing.

This is a very smooth trip. Only just now that we have come through the Tsugaru-kaikyo from the Sea of Japan into the Pacific is there a very slight roll. Unfortunately it is misty so we haven't been able to see anything except a faint mountainous outline.

It hasn't been a bit hot since we got on board but at all meals except one the air conditioning in the dining room has been on at its coldest. Our table is right in the path of a blower and even if the food is boiling hot when it is brought to us, by the time I get it up to my mouth it is ice cold. At lunch today the head waitress came to tell us the sad news that the freezing ice box had broken so the ice cream had spoiled. I said I wished the air conditioning machine would break, which was considered a big joke, and she said she would tell the manager. She came back later saying, "I have arranged for it to be broken," and at the next meal it was much warmer.

We have had salad made of seaweed which was quite good though rubbery, and shark's fin soup which I don't like.

🐚 nine

July 27, Hotel Okura, Tokyo

On the dot again we arrived at Yokohama as scheduled, at exactly four o'clock. The Trumbulls were waiting for us with a car. We drove through Yokohama, on a new thruway-type road to Tokyo and I never once felt I was in Japan. It was like a highway anywhere, most especially like the United States. I had imagined that during our boat trip down the Japanese coast we would see storybook scenery, all mouth-watering colors of mountains and beautiful ocean, pretty boats with fishermen, and villages nestled here and there, and that when we landed there would be more beautiful colors and Fujiyama in the distance looking white and pink and heavenly the way it does in pictures, and that we would drive on small streets lined with wood houses all just like the one that was in the garden of the Museum of Modern Art in New York several years ago.

But no. First of all there was a record-breaking fog during most of our time on the sea and we saw nothing but a little bit of water and mist; as we sailed into the harbor all I could see were smoke stacks belching pollution just like Con Edison on the East River; cranes, oil tanks, machinery, coal, hundreds of freighters, well-worn and shabby; nothing but industry, not a pleasure boat in sight; no color, even the water is gray-brown. It seemed like a conglomerate port-city of the worst parts of New York, New Jersey and Los Angeles.

But now I feel better about Tokyo than I did at first. We have a big room on the tenth floor of this hotel, the service is perfect and we are very comfortable. From the window nothing looks especially Japanese. The Tokyo tower is exactly like the Eiffel tower and among the characterless buildings we can spot only one group of wooden houses huddled together in one small block. What I have seen is either interesting or beautiful or both, and I shall forget about the rest of the city which is so much like Los Angeles. It is awfully clean for a huge city and yet it is so crowded with traffic I don't see how they sweep the streets. During World War II we bombed Tokyo almost to oblivion and there is very little of the old city left. Fortunately a few areas escaped and here and there one finds traditional Japanese wooden houses set in a compound with gardens and lawns, all opening off narrow, winding streets with high walls. There are gates in the walls and occasionally you can see through an open one to a charming doorway or stone path or steps.

Most of the temples and shrines have been destroyed by fire many times. For instance, the Asakusa Kannon Temple has burned thirty times since it was founded in the fourteenth century, the last during World War II. Leading up to this temple is the Nakamise Arcade with little shops on both sides, selling kimonos, parasols, every kind of souvenir, and beautiful ornaments made of rhinestones, hair clips, tiaras and necklaces. It is crowded and busy and noisy and reminded me of the pagodas in Burma except that here it is flat, there are no steps. Two giant figures stand at the gate, and enormous paper lanterns, fluted and painted, hang under the roof. There are fountains with dippers for people to rinse their mouths and wash their hands before entering the temple and stacks of incense burning in a huge container, the smoke blowing around deliciously. While a few people fold their hands and are quiet for a moment in front of the Buddha, most of them seem to be sightseers and most are Japanese.

I went to the Meiji Shrine which is breath-takingly beautiful. It is my imagined ideal of Japanese architecture, use of space, of planting, of color, or lack of color, of simplicity and perfection. I walked on the wide gravel paths through the huge gates and as I made the last turn there was this lovely sight. It is all natural wood, darkened by time (and not very much time; this, too was damaged in the war and was not completely rebuilt until 1958), with some carving and white painted accents, but everything is under-stated, subtle and beautiful. Two or three young monks in white robes completed the perfect harmony.

I have also been to a department store and taken a ride in the subway. The store was like a combination of Macy's and Saks Fifth Avenue and was full of well-dressed Japanese, most dressed in our kind of clothes, not in kimonos. Everything I looked at was of good quality and the prices were not cheap. I could hardly tear myself away from the expensive kimono department; it was more like a museum than a store. I hadn't realized that several kimonos are often worn at the same time or that a woman's undermost kimono is apt to be so pretty, of eyelet or delicate thin cotton. The Japanese department stores are famous for their wares and also because they have art galleries on a par with regular and museum galleries. Riding on the Tokyo subway is a revelation to any one who is used to the dirt and drab of the New York City subways. The platforms and cars are as clean as a first class hotel lobby. The ventilation is excellent and the seats are covered with bright blue plush that looked as if it had just been vacuumed and brushed. I didn't see any papers or trash on the floor, either in the cars or on the platform. The only fault I can find is the noise; it is incredible and it is not possible to talk with anyone. But this is summer and the windows are open; perhaps when they are closed it is quieter.

This morning I looked out of the window and saw two girls near the pool with their shirts hanging loose, outside their skirts, and later in the street I noticed many women dressed in the same way. I thought, "Heavens, so many pregnant women—about one in three—what a population explosion," until Jean Trumbull told me that this is the customary dress for most working girls and women.

This afternoon we are going to Kyoto for one night and a day, not long enough but better than nothing.

July 29, Tokyo, Noon

WE RETURNED from Kyoto last night after a visit which, though far too brief, did give us a unique and personal look at real Japanese life—something we might never have known. Wednesday at four we took the famous bullet train which can travel at a speed of 150 miles per hour, though the fastest we saw recorded on a speedometer in the dining car was 135 miles per hour. We raced through the beautiful countryside with scarcely a bump, able to see as far as our eyes could reach, through the huge windows on either side. The conductors wore spotless tan uniforms, the seats had clean covers of the same color, and everything looked cool and immaculate. It seems absurd for the United States not to have trains like this. It would be so much less trouble than airplanes for short trips and far more pleasant than driving oneself or going by bus. It seems very short-sighted to me for us to have more and more people with more and more cars, needing more and more roads when most of our cities are impossible to get in and out of comfortably as it is, and the existing highways are often jammed. I knew a lady who said she was glad she'd be dead before our country was solid cement. She is dead now, and just about in time, if you look at places like Long Island. With railroad beds and tracks all established, how simple it would be to put some new life into them rather than make all our transportation dependent on cars and roads. Some-times it seems as if General Motors and the cement industry run the country.

As so often it has been for us, the clouds hung low and thick and we couldn't see Mt. Fujiyama, but we are always so thankful when it isn't raining we can't complain about anything else. What we did see was green, and more green, all shades. There is the brightness of the rice, the deeper green of the evergreens and varying shades in between. Everything is small and contained and worked over, the same as the Italian landscape, or that of any small country where there can be no waste; every inch is planned for and used accordingly. Occasionally we saw the ocean, beyond the gray, volcanic rocks.

We left on the dot and arrived on the dot (in Japan everything is on time, too), and Ernest Satow met us. His wife is the ninth generation of the family which has owned the Tawaraya Inn for all those years. He is half Japanese and half American. When we got to know him better I said it must be awful to be that mixture—we are so different in every way—and he said, "It is." For instance, he was a boy in Tokyo during the war. But difficult as it may have been for him, it must have been terrible for his American mother. What conflicts she must have suffered. I wonder whom she thought of as the enemy.

Other people, especially Elizabeth Vining, have written of the delights of staying at the Tawaraya Inn; how the household is lined up outside the door to greet you, bowing and smiling; how, as you step out of your shoes and into slippers, you step out of your everyday life and into a world of beauty and serenity. Our special maid led us to our rooms, a living room with a sofa, two chairs and a table, two other rooms and a bathroom. All had windows opening onto private gardens. I said to Harrison, "At last, here is the kind of house that was at the Museum of Modern Art," and it turns out that the architect who remodeled the Inn did the house, Mr. Yoshimura.

We freshened up and our smiling maid led us up two flights to the roof where we had a drink and looked down on and over the gardens and the surrounding roofs. The roof-top was small; it had a chin-high wall on two sides, the wall of the house on another; a low table covered with bright red felt, used as a table or for sitting on, a big red parasol in the corner, and on the fourth side a low wall we could sit on, and beyond it a garden of stones and green plants on the flat roof of, I think, our rooms. Here, in the middle of a city block, was peace and calm and beauty, and though everything was small, there was no feeling of being cramped, only of space, exquisitely arranged.

We had dinner at a restaurant a brisk ten-minute walk from the Inn. Brisk is an odd word to use in the heat of Asia, but over and over again on this trip where it has been just *so* hot the native people walk very fast, yet they never seem to be overheated. I think I walk fast but many times I have found myself lagging on behind, conscious of making an effort to keep up. Harrison never hurries and never seems to be walking briskly, but he has an even pace for doing everything and with his long, easy stride is always out in front. The only time I think I may have done better was walking down some of those wet and muddy mountain sides in Sikkim, when a halting, cautious step meant less slipping and stumbling.

The restaurant was beside the river and we dined by candlelight outdoors on a terrace with the soft wind blowing on us. This was our first experience sitting on the floor. It is awfully uncomfortable after a while and I had to keep shifting my aching, aging bones but I imagine, like everything, if we did it all the time we wouldn't notice it. Our dinner was cooked on a burner in the middle of the table by a beautiful waitress who knelt at the end of the table and kept a constant watch on our plates and bowls and glasses. Everything was cooked for a few minutes in a broth that got better and better and we drank it as we ate all the wonderful pieces of meat and vegetables and unknown concoctions. After dinner we walked around the city for a while. The streets are narrow and the houses and shops spill out into the streets which are crowded with people, bicycles, motorcycles plus many small Japanese cars and a few larger. It made me think of Florence and how full of everything those streets get at times and how much noise there is until the jam is cleared away—often by a car having to back up out of the street, abandoning all hope of getting through.

Back at the Inn our beds were made in the bigger room with two windows on the garden. Mattresses are laid on the floor and made up just like comfortable beds anywhere but somehow it seems more seductive than regular beds with headboards and legs. We washed and rinsed outside the deep wooden tub, then got in and soaked in the hottest water we could stand, the way the Japanese do.

At nine o'clock Thursday morning we started out and went first to what our host calls the street of one hundred houses. It is inhabited by families who have been weaving beautiful materials for generations. The handlooms and machines are either in the house or adjoining buildings and in the past the whole family worked at the business. Weaving silk and damask by hand is slow and exacting, an art that seems doomed to disappear, for most young people don't want to be bothered. A finished obi, or sash, requires so many hours of painstaking work, one can cost up to $500. Most of the weavers we saw were quite old men.

We drove out to the country, although only about twenty minutes away, to a temple in a setting of high, straight trees with sunlight filtering delicately down onto the moss and stones. We walked up a steep paved path, up steps to a walk of large square stones placed in a diamond pattern with a stone lantern at each side. From there, steps lead straight up the mountain to a small temple on top and the main buildings are off to the right where there is a perfect garden in a perfect setting. This was a wonderful example of the Japanese effort to make houses and temples and gardens a part of, or extension of, nature, with nothing clashing, nothing either subduing or conquering, everything in harmony. We looked at the garden and saw how it was planned with the mountains in the background and the shapes and proportions and arrangements of the plants were just that, a part of the distance and beautiful view, yet close and intimate.

We drove out further to a village where everyone works at or in the lumber business. It is very profitable and each family owns a car. A sparkling river runs through this town in the midst of mountains, steep and high, with narrow valleys, so like Vermont. In fact this part of Japan makes me think of New England; the landscape is on a so much smaller scale than what we have seen recently. The forests in these mountains are completely managed; every inch is under control. Strips of trees are cut; after they are cleared away, new trees are planted. These are carefully tended and pruned and cut at different stages—some when tall, young, spindly saplings, another batch when large enough for boards, and some left until the size for beams and gates. We watched a girl strip the bark off a cedar sapling; she loosened it at the cut end with a blunt wood instrument and peeled it off up to the few branches left at the top. The bark is tied into packages to be used for roofs, etc., and the young trees are leaned up against the houses in the sun to dry. The top foliage is left on to draw up the moisture so the wood will dry out quicker and more evenly. Another step is to rub the wood with fine sand to make it smooth.

The houses and store houses for lumber are built on either side of the river with foot bridges across it at intervals. The stripping and drying and polishing are done at the houses and the sawing at the buildings and yards used only for lumber. While it is a big profitable business, it is handled in such small scale individual operations, it is like a series of home industries rather than a lumber business. In this village we saw many flowers growing in tiny gardens, in pots, in windows, as one sees in Switzerland, and children playing in the river and trying to catch trout with their hands.

We followed a big highway through the mountains. While this is a new road and not entirely landscaped yet, we could see it will be beautiful (though I hate to see highways slashed out of mountains anywhere; I still think they should be left with only trails and if people want to get to the top, they should walk). Many young trees were set out all along and banks were planted with small trees and shrubs. So many countries we have visited are having great tree-planting projects. In India there were many with either wood or brick cages built around the young trees to protect them from the animals, but, unfortunately, we often saw cows eating the tops of trees that had managed to survive and poke a few branches up out of the protective surrounding. In Sikkim many new trees had been set out along the roads, in Ulan Bator every street and new construction had planting, and in Siberia everywhere we went there were hundreds of newly-planted trees.

Back in town we had lunch at a restaurant looking out on an all green garden with water running through it. Again we sat on the floor and a lovely lady in a thin black kimono knelt at the table and gave us the most beautiful food I have ever seen. As soon as we had arrived we were given tiny glasses of a plum liqueur with ice—delicious and refreshing. Just before we began our meal Ernest and our waitress had a very lively talk and I said, "Japanese is a wonderful language, you always sound as if you were talking about the most exciting thing in the world." He replied, "We were, we were talking about the trout we are going to have for lunch."

Before the trout we had hors d'oeuvres, thin slices of a mysterious unknown vegetable lightly covered with sauce and served in a glass dish set in ice, which was shaved until it was like snow and heaped in a big mound on a tray—one for each of us. Also placed in the snow was a glass of beer and chopsticks and a spray of green leaves on top. Abalone and lettuce soup, prawns with glutenous rice, a trough-like dish made of bamboo filled with shrimp, noodles, egg and mushrooms followed, and after all that, as if we hadn't already had enough, a small glazed brazier with tiny pieces of hot charcoal burning inside was given to each of us, and a plate of marinated beef strips, mushrooms and onions, for us to cook for ourselves. Dessert was melon, the only thing we ate with a spoon. We had tea and beer at intervals. Somehow or other we never felt full or that there was too much; each new dish was an exciting event and a creation of beauty. So much care and artistry goes into everything these people do. I realize that most Japanese people don't live like this every day, but this is their style, their tradition, to make so much of the smallest details of living.

After lunch we went to see the Ryoanzi Temple with its famous Zen garden of stones in sand, enclosed by an old wall. It looks more like water than land; the sand is raked into neat lines every morning and the large stones emerge like continents in an ocean. Beyond the wall are huge pine trees reaching way up into the sky so that you get the feeling of infinity wherever you look. This temple is simple and lovely and is situated just up from an artificial lake with mountains in the background. Years ago a man created the lake to reflect the mountains, so, as his house was next to the lake just below the temple, he could see the mountains in the water from his entrance—he didn't have to walk to have a view. Thus he brought the nature that he wanted into his house.

We visited a beautiful small temple where our hosts were married. This seemed less formal, more homelike and personal than most. The chief monk is married and his wife brought us cold tea. From the steps of the main building we gazed at a garden of only maple trees with a stone lantern in the middle. Beyond this was a more formal arrangement of shrubs and water in a little stream, and as always, stones. The monk showed us all the rooms in the temple and brought out two Chinese paintings—so old and so valuable they are reputed to be the reason Kyoto wasn't bombed during World War II—and lovingly unrolled them and hung them up for us to see. He walked with us to an outer gate, a sign that we were honored guests. These gestures of politeness, of consideration and appreciation, are disarming and so appealing.

Back at the Inn we had another bath, got ready to leave and sat in our own Japanese living room and talked about our day. We both felt it was a work of art—a beautifully planned and charmingly carried out series of glimpses into real Japanese life—examples of contemporary living with their historic background. Although at one point I thought I didn't want to go to Japan, that I had had enough travelling and wasn't in the mood for another new, strange country, how glad I will always be that we came. It is so entirely different from the last few countries we have been in, it is a perfect place to end our trip. It has been stimulating, refreshing and relaxing all at one. While I feel there is a formality and coolness here which would prevent me from ever feeling really "with" the Japanese, I am fascinated by their approach to life and utterly charmed with the thought and care they put into everything, and the beauty and style they achieve.

This afternoon I will buy a few last presents to take home, pack my poor old clothes I am so tired of for the last time, and we leave at eight. We fly nearly nine hours without stopping, straight across the Pacific to San Francisco. There, if all goes well, we will have seats to New York. There is an airplane strike in the United States but evidently some planes are still flying.

It is strange to think this long, long trip is nearly over. We have been so far, seen so much, met so many people, everything and everyone different, and yet not different. If there is a final conclusion to be drawn, it is just that. We have talked to different types of people in different countries with different ways of living. They have different kinds of governments, different religions, different customs, different standards. What is black to some is white to others and yet fundamentally they are the same. Whether African or Asian, European or American, most human beings want the same things; peace in which to live and work and bring up their children; peace in which to raise the living standards of the poor, to fight disease, combat hunger; peace in which to come to grips with all man's problems which can never be settled by war.

♨ *ten*

July 30, New York City

EVERYTHING went smoothly. We waited several
hours in San Francisco, then flew to New York, feeling
terribly lucky to have seats. As we stumbled off the plane at
midnight Friday, New York time (Saturday noon, our
time), there were Rosina, Scott, Stephan and Curtis. What a
glorious sight to see—better than any of the last two and a
half months. We drove into town. The house is beautiful,
the cats are adorable, the garden fantastic, the wisteria has
grown up to the roof, and we are glad to be home.

New York City

WE HAVE been home for several months now and
I have finally finished making two huge scrapbooks of our

trip. They include most of the pictures we both took, maps and postcards; letters, notes and invitations from people we met at the various stops; all the articles Harrison wrote en route and the series he did when we returned. So now we have a permanent record of every aspect of this fabulous trip under one cover, or two, and we can take it as many more times as we want from the comfort of our own house.

But even sitting in front of the fire, comfortably curled up on the sofa, the cats purring beside me, I don't really need the scrapbooks to help me remember. Nothing has faded, every detail still stands out. The magic colors of Cambodia, the melee of life in the Bangkok klongs, the grace and beauty of the Southeast Asian people, the charm and fairy-tale quality of Sikkim, my surprise that Siberia was so beautiful and the people so open and friendly and independent—all the new sights and smells and sounds, all the people we met and the friends we made—everything is with me as if we were still in those countries.

I wonder if they will be able to remain Asian, to maintain their special identity, and if the rest of the world will allow them to work out their own problems in their own way. I wonder what would happen in Vietnam if we weren't there. I wonder if, left alone, they might not reach a solution that would satisfy most of the Vietnamese, though it might not satisfy Americans. What are we really doing there except trying to impose our thinking, our way of life, with our army, our bombs, our modern technology, on a small simple peasant country?

I am more convinced every day that what we are doing is wrong. The war goes on and on; our young men are wounded and dying hour after hour; the Vietnamese people, North and South, are being subjected to unimaginable suffering day after day; their country is being destroyed; and our government seems intent on continuing, prolonging, even enlarging, this terrible conflict. How can we keep on? What is anyone gaining? I wish every American could have the chance to see what I have seen, meet the people I have met, to become aware that we are one world and one people and to realize that we cannot destroy another country without, in the end, destroying ourselves.